FUNNY PEOPLE

Roy Smiles

FUNNY PEOPLE

My Journey Through Comedy

OBERON BOOKS
LONDON

WWW.OBERONBOOKS.COM

First published in 2011 by Oberon Books Ltd

521 Caledonian Road, London N7 9RH

Tel: +44 (0) 20 7607 3637 / Fax: +44 (0) 20 7607 3629

e-mail: info@oberonbooks.com

www.oberonbooks.com

A catalogue record for this book is available from the British Library.

ISBN: 978-1-84943-034-0

Cover photography by Nobby Clark

Cover design by James Illman

Printed in Great Britain by CPI Antony Rowe, Chippenham

'The tragedy of men is that they live in this ghastly wasteland of second-hand jokes' – Jonathan Miller.

CONTENTS

Introduction

**'There are three rules of comedy.
One: there are no rules of comedy...
Two: you weren't listening to the first rule...
Three: what are you, deaf?' – Anon.**

Legend has it that renowned Shakespearean actor Sir Henry Irving's last words were: 'Dying is easy, comedy is hard.' Though it would be nice to think it was actually true he probably had more pressing concerns at the time: like throwing up a lung (my favourite exit line is Oscar Wilde's death-bed quip: 'either me or these curtains have to go', just as improbable but funnier). But indeed comedy is hard. My brief attempt to do stand-up comedy in the Eighties ended on one memorable night in Balham at the Banana Cabaret when I arrived to do a gig from Brighton, was told I was late and was first on, rushed on to the stage and promptly forgot my act, my name and my reason for being so quit that night, preferring the gentler pastures of playwriting.

'What's a writer but a schmuck with a typewriter?' – Harry Cohn.

The critics since have been occasionally unkind but they've never actually thrown things at me (a paper plate with a tomato on it winged its merry way towards me at Jongleurs in Battersea). Nor do they heckle me on or yell 'fuck off big nose' as I take to the stage (my response to that particular heckle was an undignified: 'fuck you', to which the female heckler responded: 'why me?' When the heckler is funnier than the act on stage it's time to call it a day).

'I've been on the road now doing comedy twelve years so bear with me while I plaster on a fake smile and plow through this shit one more time' – Bill Hicks.

However, having now had my plays on comedians staged: Spike Milligan (*Ying Tong – A Walk With The Goons*), the Beyond The Fringe team (*Good Evening*), Monty Python (*Pythonesque*), Groucho Marx and Lenny Bruce (*Schmucks*) and a soon to be staged piece on Les Dawson (*Les Sez*); not to mention un-staged plays on Tony Hancock (*The Lad Himself*) and Joan Rivers (*Funny Girls*); as well as somewhat painfully revisiting my stand-up years in my play *Stand Up* I thought it worth writing some words on the comedy performers and comedy shows that have inspired and influenced me over the years.

'My family were evicted so many times our furniture was grey to match the colour of the pavement' – Les Dawson.

I can certainly claim to have been obsessed with comedy from an early age. I can still remember the first joke I was ever told: 'What do you call a man with jelly in one ear and custard in the other? A trifle deaf.'

Which I still like to this day though the adult variation: 'What do you call a man with jelly in one ear and custard in the other? Anything, the stupid bastard can't hear you,' also has its charms.

A deeply inept ventriloquist once came to my Infant School in West Acton and died the death of a thousand clowns as we stared at the poor, sweating oaf as he failed with alarming aplomb to make seven-year-olds laugh. One of his gags was about Danny Kaye at the London Palladium and I remember asking my father later that night who and what that was. My father pointed out that Kaye had triumphantly conquered London just after the Second World War and, as this was 1970, the poor sod who told it might want to actually update his material, especially for Infant School kids...

The second joke I remember? 'What do you get when you cross a giraffe with a hedgehog? A twenty-eight foot toothbrush.'

All my memories of childhood seem to be comedy/television related.

There were no 'blue remembered hills'. Not in West Acton anyway. A suburb so boring not even the Luftwaffe would bomb it.

The only famous person who ever lived in Acton in those days was Lionel Bart, author of *Oliver*. And he only moved there to have a massive nervous breakdown. On quiet nights, when the Central Line had stopped running, you could hear his screams.

**'I live in a neighbourhood so bad that you can get shot while getting shot'
– Chris Rock.**

No one got shot in West Acton though you could occasionally get hit over the head with a rolled up newspaper. It was Walter the Softy Central. To paraphrase the writer Spike Mullins (who wrote for Ronnie Corbett) the neighbourhood was so sissy: 'you could have a reign of terror with a balloon on a stick.'

I was brought up with my older brother and sister by my Geordie grandmother and father after my mother died. My grandmother was my father's mother-in-law so there was a row a minute but as Les Dawson once said, 'we were too happy to realise we were miserable.'

**'You can always tell when the mother-in-law's come to the door: the Alsatian starts biting its nails and the mice throw themselves on traps'
– Les Dawson.**

My family were all from Gateshead so it was lard for breakfast, dinner and tea. 'Lunch' was what other people did. My grandmother's Tyneside accent was so thick a dim-witted kid at my Junior School in Ealing asked my cousin which country she was from. 'She's a Geordie,' said my cousin. 'Is that in Russia?' was the reply. And you wonder why we lost an Empire.

'Why are Geordies such well-balanced people?
They have a chip on both shoulders' – Anon.

We lived in Acton until around 1974 and it was a house full of people, as my Aunty Thora lived with us and we had a lodger, 'Uncle Mick'; it was just like *The Waltons*, though without the denim, banjos or the dribbling village idiot Jim-Bob.

In response to President Bush's 'We need a nation closer to the
Waltons than the Simpsons':
'We're just like the Waltons. We're praying for an end to the
depression too' – Bart Simpson, *The Simpsons*.

I remember endless cowboy shows and *Watch With Mother* and Yogi Bear, to the extent I don't remember much else. My grandmother was addicted to *Crossroads*, *Coronation Street* and gin in that order. So I grew up with Noele Gordon, Ena Sharples and the smell of peppermint on an old woman's breath. Though that might have been the menthol cigarettes she chain-smoked. She smoked so much she saved up for a washing machine with her cigarette coupons. And I'm not lying.

I suppose being an old woman the easiest way to deal with kids is to plonk them in front of the TV. Trust me, I wasn't complaining and I haven't changed. I can still watch a box-set of *Monk* in a day.

There's a great scene in *The Simpsons* where Bart and Lisa try to find out who baby Maggie likes more: 'Maggie, come to the one you love,' says Lisa. Maggie goes over and hugs the TV. I guess I was that kid.

'Books are useless! I only ever read one book, 'To Kill A Mockingbird',
and it gave me absolutely no insight on how to kill mockingbirds! Sure
it taught me not to judge a man by the colour of his skin, but what good
does that do me?' – Homer Simpson, *The Simpsons*.

I was one of the few rational human beings ever to find joy in the vaguely moronic *Beverly Hillbillies*. There was *Top Cat* naturally, the animated tribute to *Bilko*, *The Flintstones* (oddly the only cartoon ever to win an Emmy, which includes *The Simpsons*, probably the greatest comedy show of all time – go figure) *The Banana Splits*, *The Munsters*, *The Addams Family*, *Rowan & Martin's Laugh In*, *Car 54 Where Are You?*, *The Mary Tyler Moore Show*, *F-Troop* – to name but a few.

Cavalry Captain to his horse-soldiers: 'Unmount!' – *F-Troop*.

Then there were the comics: Mike & Bernie Winters, Chic Murray, Dave Allen, Tony Hancock, Jimmy Tarbuck, *Sunday Night At The London Palladium*, the emerging Les Dawson. And all the old comedy movies the cheap BBC used to repeat endlessly in the school holidays: Abbott & Costello, Laurel & Hardy, George Formby, the Three Stooges, Will Hay, the dread Norman Wisdom...

I suppose I was like a sponge soaking it all up and that at the back of my mind I must have wanted to earn my living as a comic writer one day. Though, at the time, I was obsessed with cowboys and the writings of J.T. Edson, a Western writer – from Rotherham as it turned out – who wrote about Dusty Fogg, a cross-drawing midget gunslinger from Texas – well, he was short if not a midget but writing Westerns was the original plan.

So this will be my journey: to relate how comedy shows and comedians influenced and affected me in my life and how it led me to writing plays of a comedic bent; from the Marx Brothers (the sublime) to Charlie Drake (the ridiculous) via Monty Python's *Flying Circus* (the god-like) to Benny Hill (the remedial).

**Interviewer Michael Parkinson to Eric Morecambe and Ernie Wise:
'What would you have been if you hadn't been comedians?'
Eric Morecambe : '
We'd have been Mike & Bernie Winters...'**

The Childhood Years

The first show I probably remember laughing at is *Bill & Ben*, two (possibly gay) flowerpot men who talked to a plant and spoke in gibberish. I can only presume the show was written by a writer high on crack. Not that they had crack in those days. Nay, they were simpler times, save for heroin, cocaine, LSD and morphine the streets were clean of drugs.

Actually the only thing they snorted in West Acton was Bassett's Sherbet Fountain; which didn't make you high but did block your nostrils with alarming affect. I might have been vaguely addicted to the fizzy drink Tizer but that's another story for another time.

'But enough about me, more about you, what do you think of me?'
– Bette Midler.

No, Bill & Ben might have been a tad simplistic but, as I found years later with my son and *Pingu the Penguin* in the mid-Nineties, little kids will laugh at anything provided it's done with gusto.

I probably laughed at the wobbly sets of *Crossroads* at around about the same time. A soap opera of such startling ineptitude it makes *Eastenders* look professional.

In my play *Pythonesque*, about the Monty Python team (to whom I shall return), I had them waxing lyrical for that supposed Golden Age of Television the Sixties:

> *CLEESE, CHAPMAN, PALIN and IDLE sit in chairs wearing cloth caps, speaking in self-satisfied northern accents, in the style of 'The Four Yorkshiremen' sketch:*

CHAPMAN.   The Sixties, a golden age of television, not like the rubbish they put on today. People shows? If I want to watch people and be entertained I'll go to my local park and watch juvenile delinquents in hooded tops stab strangers.

PALIN.   Aye, they made proper television programmes in those days. Like *Play for Today:* they'd have a miserable play on BBC One about miserable people leading miserable lives and it'd get an audience of eighteen million – and keep those eighteen million viewers depressed for days.

CLEESE.   Aye, kitchen-sink dramas, those were the days. Some were so miserable they filmed the entire play in an actual sink, with the actors splashing around in the murky water.

IDLE.   Dealing with subjects like suicide, despair, homelessness and death by poverty; you just don't get plays on television as entertaining as that these days do you?

CHAPMAN.   No, in the Sixties on television you couldn't move for quality entertainment. Like *Pinky & Perky:* puppets of pigs singing Herman's Hermits hits at high speeds; aye, ribald satire at its best.

PALIN.   You had the *Black & White Minstrels:* racist white men with banjos, singing *Mammy* and *Camp Town Races* in blackface; you just don't get sophistication like that anymore, do you?

CLEESE.   You had *Pot Black:* snooker in black and white; watching the grey balls and the slightly darker grey balls being pocketed by chain-smoking drunkards: avid viewing.

IDLE.   *Bonanza:* the Western series about a gay fifty-year old rancher and his three gay forty-seven year old sons: always believable.

PALIN.	*Coronation Street:* and its honest, gritty depiction of fat-arsed, repulsive men and bandy-legged, repulsive women.
CHAPMAN.	*The Forsythe Saga:* the costume drama that made wife-beating fashionable again.
CLEESE.	And the stand-up club comedians: bloated bigots in tuxedo doing jokes about Pakistanis, black people or thick Irishmen.
PALIN.	Gleefully spreading hate, ignorance and fear under the guise of japery.
CHAPMAN.	Sneering at their wives for being ugly despite being grotesquely ugly bastards themselves.
IDLE.	Aye, Sixties television had it all.
CHAPMAN.	And *Monty Python* – lest we forget.
PALIN.	*Monty Python:* totally original.
IDLE.	Totally changed the face of comedy as we knew it.
CLEESE.	If Spike Milligan hadn't have done it first it would have been almost groundbreaking.

Alas, we never had BBC2 on our telly so I had to get impressions of Monty Python from my friends at school, who were often so convulsed by laughter you couldn't actually make out what they were saying. Except that it involved the words 'spam' or 'parrot.'

'My family were so poor we thought knives and forks were jewellery. But we had duck for Christmas, if the parks were open' – Les Dawson.

But before Python there were a legion of shows to get addicted too: there was *Hogan's Heroes*, a show set in a prisoner-of-war camp, with disturbingly loveable Nazis. *Get Smart*, a spy spoof written by Mel Brooks, which I thought hilarious at the time, but on repeat viewing as an adult I found mildly irritating. *Lost In Space*, a sci-fi show, where a very camp Dr. Zachery Smith traded quips with a surprisingly funny robot. *Bewitched,* an annoyingly cute show about witches and warlocks which seems to be recalled in fondness by my generation: despite the Vaseline in Dick York's hair. There was *The Flying Nun*, which I thought was weird shit I'd made up whilst on magic mushrooms; the young Sally Fields played a nun whose habit allowed her to fly through the city solving people's problems. I'd have loved to have been there when they pitched that particular show: 'SAY WHAT? GET THE MEDICS! HE'S ON OPIUM AGAIN!' There was *H.R. Pufnstuf,* a fantasy show set in a Never-Never Land where Jack Wild from the musical *Oliver!* hung about with giant puppets for no apparent reason; it wasn't very funny actually but I adored it and oddly it was Kurt Cobain's favourite childhood show too.

There was *The Andy Williams Show*, which is sort of remembered more now for being the show that introduced The Osmonds and their Mormon warblings to the world but was actually a very funny show and had a great running gag with a giant talking bear: 'Got any cookies Andy?' 'Not now, not ever, now never!' Actually that doesn't sound that funny but you had to be there at the time. *Basil Brush* was a scream though you always suspected the guy working him (a fox glove puppet) was half-cut on vino – and it turned out he was.

In hindsight the tragedy was the shows that didn't come over from the States. I once reduced a rehearsal room in Philadelphia to stunned silence when I told the American cast of my Groucho Marx/Lenny Bruce play *Schmucks* the BBC had never shown *The Tonight Show* when I was young, or at all come to think of it. 'No Carson?' said one of the actors. 'What the hell did you do at night?' 'We had sex,' I quipped. We never got the *Carol Burnett Show* or *The Dean Martin Show* either (not that I recall); which was a shame when you see all the brilliant clips on YouTube now.

'You're not drunk if you can lie on the floor without holding on' – Dean Martin.

We did get *Rowan & Martin's Laugh-In*, the hip late Sixties show that introduced Goldie Hawn to a grateful world. The show was a blast.

An updating of *Hellzapoppin'* for the Swinging Sixties scene:

'Solomon Grundy, by Henry Gibson; Solomon Grundy born on Monday; went to school on Tuesday; grew a beard on Wednesday; expelled on Thursday; protested on Friday; arrested on Saturday; drafted on Sunday; and this was the end of Solomon Grundy'
– Henry Gibson, *Rowan and Martin's Laugh-In*.

Though it wore its liberalism openly on its sleeve it didn't stop them having Richard Nixon on the show yelling 'sock it to me!' (Without actually knowing what he was talking about) and John Wayne sending up his own image with the poem: 'The sky is blue, the grass is green; get off of your butts and join the Marines!'

'The preceding was recorded earlier because we were ashamed to do it now'
– Announcer, *Rowan & Martin's Laugh-In*.

It seems from the above paragraphs I was living in Ohio rather than West Acton but the BBC did tend to import a lot of American shows in those days. The one British comedy show that was repeated ad-infinitum all through my early years was *Hancock's Half Hour*. It was a particular favourite of my grandmother's. Years later I wrote the play *The Lad Himself* in tribute. I think my grandmother being from Gateshead she shared Hancock's melancholy and somewhat obstreperous anti-establishment attitude:

HANCOCK.   'Margate, lovely, lovely Margate, city of love and laughter; see the majestic, toilet-roll strewn beaches; as far as the eye can see bandy-legged locals awash with sun cream, hog the towels stolen as recently as this morning from their local B & B, in between urinating in the sea and dodging unexploded World War II mines. And there's Butlin's – that hastily converted concentration camp without the guard dogs or barbed wire but with Charlie Chester doing the cabaret which is worse; ah Margate, where they don't bury the dead – they elect them councillors; on a clear day you can see the nuclear power plant. See the Teddy Boys, gallantly helping the elderly deckchair attendant with his round, before beating him to a merry pulp for his small change. See the children splashing in the rust-coloured ocean. Wrestling happily with the local friendly shark; oops, there goes another leg. See their genial, twinkle-eyed grandparents, rifling their grandkids possessions as they swim; and there's the local trollop Gladys; giving the Royal Navy their traditional send-off, behind the bike sheds. But we journey away from the beaches to move inland. Ah, Margate High Street: Paradise once removed. There's Boots, Woolworths, that shop with the surgical gadgets no one ever talks about; the local Bobby on his beat, that traditional English sight, ruffling the hair of passing urchins whilst taking large bribes from the cheery neighbourhood pimp; see the rosy-cheeked district nurse, Winifred, arse the size of Burnley, peddling her push-bike like the hordes of Hades are behind her, giggling like a banshee. Yes, she's been at the morphine again. See the ivy covered tea-rooms and their traditional fare of jam, scone and salmonella; see the red phone-boxes smelling of tramp wee and the local farmer going about his busy day – strangling badgers; yes, the sights and sounds of dearest, dearest Blighty. Just turn left at France and follow the smell of chip fat' – The Lad Himself.

Performing in a weekly revue show on radio Hancock was lucky enough to be paired with two up-and-coming comedy writers who'd met on a TB ward: Ray Galton and Alan Simpson. It was a match made in heaven. The Hancock of Galton & Simpson's making was a sort of pompous Everyman, constantly at odds with his world and the reality of his delusions (an extension of Hancock's real personality as it happens).

Starting off with support from Kenneth Williams, Hattie Jacques, the Australian Bill Kerr and the cockney-South African Sid James the show became a massive hit and eventually transferred to television.

Ditching Williams, Jacques and Kerr with blithe indifference Hancock with James as his shifty, womanising foil made one of the first great British comedy television shows. Eventually tiring of being a double act with James he ditched Sid as well (an act of career suicide that stands up there with Morecambe & Wise going to ITV).

But the six episodes he made on his own were the finest shows he did: including *The Radio Ham*, *The Lift*, The *Bedsitter*, *The Bowman's* (a glorious parody of the dull rural radio serial *The Archers*) and, of course, the famous *The Blood Donor*.

The story of his alcoholic self-destruction and suicide at forty-four is well known. But rather than get immersed in tears of clown clichés let's remember a man who brought pleasure to millions and emptied the pubs when his show was on.

**'Does Magna Carta mean nothing to you? Did she die in vain?'
– Tony Hancock.**

In my Hancock play he's committed suicide and arrives in Limbo to be judged; only to find the same bureaucracy and officialdom he found on earth, that God is indeed a woman and that Limbo is the waiting room from *The Blood Donor*:

> *HANCOCK enters through the double doors of a hospital waiting room. He is dressed in a grey Macintosh and Trilby hat. He stops, sighs and looks around him sourly. The music fades. The waiting room is empty save for a VICAR (in the style of Hugh Lloyd) reading a Bible.*

HANCOCK. Marvellous. *(Beat)* All this way for this. *(Beat)* Dear-oh-dear. *(To Vicar)* This is it, is it?

VICAR. I beg your pardon?

HANCOCK. This is it, is it, the afterlife, a hospital waiting room?

VICAR. Yes, I believe so.

HANCOCK. I see. *(Beat)* If they ask me to give blood they'll be trouble. It's not right. *(Beat)* Where's the welcoming committee then?

VICAR. Welcoming committee?

HANCOCK.	Made up of Marco Polo, Wyatt Earp and the deck-hands of *The Titanic*.
VICAR.	I'm not with you.
HANCOCK.	Where's the celestial host greeting me in all their majesty? Playing those harps like whirling dervishes and flapping their wings like banshees?
VICAR.	I don't think you get that. No, not at all, you just wait to be judged.
HANCOCK.	Charming. *(Beat)* I expected more than this I can tell you. Where's the male voice choirs, the legions of white clad minstrels doing the great hymns of our time, where's Mary Magdalene and her foot wash? *(Beat)* You'd think with the body God gave me he'd be here to apologize.
VICAR.	I'd keep your voice down, you know. You don't want to get into any trouble.
HANCOCK.	Come, come sir: I'm brown bread, a corpse, pushing up the daisies, food for the worms; my ashes soon to be the contents of a glorified ashtray. How much trouble can I get into?
VICAR.	We're all dead but one mustn't rock-the-boat.
HANCOCK.	Oh, mustn't one, and how very lily-livered of you to say so, sir.
VICAR.	I was just saying –
HANCOCK.	Yes, I know what you were saying. I met a lot of your sort during the war. Oh yes, I know your type right enough. Lick-spittle's all.
VICAR.	I am not a lick-spittle. I just happen to want to get into heaven with the minimum of fuss.
HANCOCK.	How do you know you'll be getting into heaven? That's a bit smug isn't it?
VICAR.	What do you mean?
HANCOCK.	You might well have been rifling the collection plate like a Grammar School cad for all I know.
VICAR.	*(Offended)* I do not rifle collection plates.

HANCOCK. You might have been at the communion wine. You look a tippler.

VICAR. How dare you.

HANCOCK. You'll find no Gods in the bottom of a glass, mate. I should know. What happened? Get pissed and fall out of your pulpit?

VICAR. This is outrageous.

HANCOCK. You should have soaked the grog up with some communion wafer. Jesus may have turned water into wine but he didn't say drink *Oddbins* dry.

VICAR. I am not a drunk. As it happens I died peacefully in my sleep. Now will you please keep your voice down?

HANCOCK. They could have sent a welcoming committee that's all I'm saying.

VICAR. Why on earth would they send you, of all people, a welcoming committee?

HANCOCK. I'm not your common throng. I'm something of a celebrity. I had a dash of greatness about me. All the reviewers said so.

VICAR. Greatness? *(Mocking laugh) You*?

HANCOCK. You're toying with me, sir. Surely you must recognise me.

VICAR. Not in the least.

HANCOCK. What's the matter, never have a telly?

VICAR. As a matter of fact I didn't.

HANCOCK. A radio, then, I was huge on the radio.

VICAR. I didn't have a radio either.

HANCOCK. *(Stares)* What are you, Amish?

VICAR. I happen to be C of E.

HANCOCK. Ah, yes. The religion that thinks God is white, middle class and a dead ringer for Kenneth More; atheism with hymns, that's your lot.

VICAR. Will you keep your voice down? Remember where you are. They won't take kindly to assaults on organized religion here.

HANCOCK.	Oh, get back to your Bible. What you reading it for anyway? Looking for loop holes?
VICAR.	Well really –
HANCOCK.	Yes, yes, get back to Solomon sawing babies in half.

Thought it was written brilliantly by Galton & Simpson, I never took to *Steptoe & Son*, I always found it deeply depressing. So Pinteresque even Pinter was slashing his wrists while watching. The story of a father and son running a rag-and-bone business has legendary status and in Harry H. Corbett you have one of the finest actors ever to bestride a comedy show but the gloominess of the situation and scripts made me depressed even as a child.

But from the despairing to the exhilarating: let's talk cartoons, folks!

'What an embezzle! What an ultramaroon!' – Bugs Bunny

Now Bugs Bunny, I know he's a corporate whore for Warner Brothers these days, but he was in many ways the Groucho Marx for my generation and my father's before me, the Forties Bugs Bunny cartoons being gloriously well written. *What's Opera Doc* won a deserved Oscar for its parody of Wagnerian pomposity.

'Goodbye, and don't think it hasn't been a little slice of heaven, 'cause it hasn't' – Bugs Bunny.

Bugs took on authority with a Brooklynesque swagger and I always thought of Elmer Fudd and Yosemite Sam as members of the National Rifle Association who deserved all the humiliation and pain Bugs could inflict on them.

Though I might suggest that generally the animators at Warner Brothers overdid Bugs' cross-dressing a tad. Another episode, another bonnet, another smacker on the lips for Elmer...

Daffy Duck was a scream too, again in the Forties originals. The episode where he's a bell-boy who can't shut up and keeps getting Elmer Fudd, as the hotel clerk, pummelled by a violent guest trying to sleep is a classic.

'Consequences, Schmonsequences, as long as I'm rich' – Daffy Duck.

I always loved Foghorn Leghorn, the loud-mouthed cowardly rooster; it was one of my nicknames at school actually as like Foghorn I had a total inability to stop talking at any moment of time, usually during lessons:

> **LEGHORN: Looky here, son, I'm no loud-mouthed schnook.** *(Slaps BARNYARD DAWG violently)* **This is a dog, not a chicken. Chickens don't look like dogs. Who told you this was a chicken, son? Nice boy, but doesn't listen to a thing you say. You got a bum steer, son. I'm a chicken, not a schnook. You're wrong, son.**
>
> **BARNYARD DAWG:** *(Kicks FOGHORN violently)* **Schnook!**
>
> **– Foghorn Leghorn**

Growing up with *Top Cat* and *Bugs Bunny* and *Foghorn* in many ways I was ingesting the vaudeville/burlesque comics they were based on. I was laughing at Top Cat years before I saw *Bilko* and found out it was based on Phil Silvers' persona.

'A sucker's groan is music to a gambler's ear'
– Bilko, *The Phil Silvers Show*.

As we mentioned it I must say a quick word about the *Phil Silvers Show*, otherwise known as 'Bilko', about a conniving, fast-talking sergeant, as played by vaudeville veteran Phil Silvers, which was made in the Fifties but repeated at length on the BBC from the Sixties onwards.

I must have been six or so when I first saw the show. I can remember the episode. It was 'The Eating Contest' and Fred Gwynne (Herman Munster from *The Munsters*) played the champion eater of the company. But he could only eat when he was depressed and heart-broken, thus Silvers spent the whole episode trying to keep him from re-uniting with his girlfriend.

The acting from much of the cast, recruited on Silver's insistence from retired sportsmen and ex-boxers (he was a fanatical gambler in real life, which led him to bankruptcy and worse later in life) was ropey at best and Paul Ford, as Colonel Hall, couldn't remember his lines if his life depended on it but the writing by Nat Hiken was exquisite and the episode where a chimp is accidentally enrolled in the army ('The Court Martial') and they have to court-martial it to get it out is a classic. At one stage, during the court-room scene, the monkey picks up the phone and Silvers defending him in court ad-libs: 'you see he's calling another lawyer!' Lovely stuff...

But let us leave behind us the windswept years of the swinging Sixties.

For the only thing that swung in the Sixties in our house was the cat, my Dad used to swing it to prove there wasn't enough room, and let us journey forth to the Seventies, a decade with all the charm of a rancid armpit. There awash in skinhead gob and charming National Front election broadcasts I came of age, in comedy as of life.

But before that, dear reader, indulge me a minor detour to the glories of... the wireless.

'Needle nardle noo' – Neddie Seagoon.

Skip forward many years to 2002 and I'm slumped in my own filth in glorious, downtown Balham (that suburb haunts me) with the charming playwright/director Terry Johnson, bemoaning the fact I'd been writing fringe plays for twelve years and getting good reviews but with average audiences you could squeeze into a phone-box and who'd still have room to take advantage of themselves.

'Why don't you write something people actually want to see?' says Johnson, my theatrical Yoda. 'That's a good idea,' says I. 'I've always wanted to write about the Goons.' 'Then bloody do it,' he said. 'And I'll direct it.' Thus I did, and he didn't.

'Aardvark never killed anyone' – Spike Milligan.

What can you say about the Goons? 'The Goons make life worth living,' John Lennon said and it was true. Ever since I could remember my uncles had done Bluebottle voices. I thought that was the way drunken Geordies spoke at weddings. Who knew?

Actually I knew as Radio 2 used to repeat the shows at dinner-time on a Sunday. My brother got the scripts when they were printed and I ended up asking for records of their shows when I was old enough to realise how good they were. I had 'The Flying Naafi' episode on vinyl and also 'The Dreaded Batter Pudding Thrower (Of Bexhill-On-Sea)' amongst others.

The Goons were made by World War Two, the total madness of that bloodbath and the absurdity of being in a British Army run by incompetent Colonel Blimps who couldn't run a piss up in a brewery let alone a modern army.

'World War Two was declared and the neighbours panicked
and took in the washing' – Spike Milligan.

Milligan met Harry Secombe in the service after he had been hospitalised for cracking up after being shelled and wounded in Italy.

He had been mentioned for bravery in dispatches in North Africa but the Italian front and being shelled by German mortars was a campaign too far. Bleeding and wounded he went to a dressing station only to be accused of cowardice by a boorish, upper-class Major. And they wondered why he had mental problems for the rest of his days?

I wrote *Ying Tong – A Walk With The Goons* and it went all around the world. The best night of my life was when the show opened at Sydney Opera House in Australia and the sold-out audience went mad, with standing ovations galore.

It was a show about Milligan's struggle to overcome his first massive breakdown whilst writing the Goon Show. So it was two hours set in a psychiatrist hospital. After the show Milligan's brother came up to me, slightly the worse for alcoholic wear, and said in all seriousness: 'My brother was quite mad, you know...' As the show had been entirely about that I could only think: 'no shit Sherlock...'

Actually the Milligan and Secombe families were great about the show, hugely supportive, which was a relief. No one from Peter Sellers' family saw it alas. But, as Mr. Sellers was never that great a father, this is hardly surprising.

To remind the audience of the show I opened *Ying Tong* with a supposed scene from the radio show and had Milligan have his break down on air. It wasn't true but set the tone and audiences liked the tribute immensely:

As the lights rise Wallace GREENSLADE, Peter SELLERS, Spike MILLIGAN and Harry SECOMBE stand at microphones, scripts in hand. A Goon Show, we presume, is about to begin.

GREENSLADE. This is the BBC Home Service.

FX: the scream of falling bombs.

SELLERS. *(Bloodnok voice)* They'll never take me alive I tell you!

GREENSLADE. Once more with feeling: this is the BBC Home Service.

MILLIGAN. *(Yells)* Abandon license fee! Women and children first!

FX: the sound of a ship's horn sounding an urgent 'abandon ship' alert.

GREENSLADE. Yes, for the last time this evening at popular prices, that acceptable face of sadism: the Goon Show.

FX: mass booing from football terraces.

GREENSLADE. How vulgar the common swineherd.

SECOMBE. Don't talk about BBC producers that way, Wal. You know they bear a grudge.

GREENSLADE. I shall grovel later. But to our sorry tale; episode one: War & Peas.

Music: a dramatic 'War & Peace' style Hollywood swell.

GREENSLADE. Somewhere midst the windswept hovels of Swansea, a myopic blubber of fat from Wales, attempting to support his illegal addiction to meat pasties, sells second-hand leeks to passing charabancs.

SECOMBE. *(Sings to the tune of 'Who Will Buy')*

'Who will buy a second-hand leek, boy?

Such a leek I never did see

Who will buy a second hand leek, boy?

And stuff it in their gob for me?'

SELLERS. *(Bluebottle voice)* Would you mind taking your hand out of your pocket whilst you warble please, genial Seagoon person? I'm trying to pick it; for I am thruppence short for my wine-gums.

SECOMBE. Bluebottle!

SELLERS. *(Bluebottle voice)* Yes, it is I. Strikes defiant Alan Ladd pose and waits for spontaneous wave of audience love. Not a sausage; sheds a silent tear.

SECOMBE. But – wait – what are you doing waving that white flag?

SELLERS. *(Bluebottle voice)* Surrendering; I am a conscientious objector from the Boy Scout movement. They've stripped me of my woggle: the dirty rotten swines.

SECOMBE. Why are you surrendering from the Boy Scout movement?

SELLERS. *(Bluebottle voice)* I started a camp fire by rubbing two sticks repeatedly against my knees. It set light to my legs.

SECOMBE. Ye Gads! What happened?

SELLERS. *(Bluebottle voice)* They had to beat out the flames with a Girl Guide. Yet they still refused to give me my pyromaniac badge. The Scout Movement are lions led by donkeys I tell you. I curse the day I ever dobbed my dib.

SECOMBE.   How fascinating yet at the same time – tedious.
But who's that jabbering ninny idly warming marshmallows on the dying embers of your kneecaps?

SELLERS.   *(Bluebottle voice)* Why that's my very good friend Eccles. Tee-hee.

MILLIGAN.   *(Eccles voice)* Hello there!

SECOMBE.   Eccles, eh? I observed a man who but for a village would be its idiot. Leave this to me: I speak fluent drivel. Tell me, young imbecile –

MILLIGAN.   *(Eccles voice)* Who you calling an imbecile? I got a diploma from borstal.

SECOMBE.   What in?

MILLIGAN.   *(Eccles voice)* Stealing.

SECOMBE.   I know I'm going to hate myself in the morning for asking this but: what are you doing with that camel?

MILLIGAN.   *(Eccles voice)* Smoking it.

SECOMBE.   Put that dromedary down, man. You don't know where it's been.

MILLIGAN.   *(Eccles voice)* I've cut down – to only three hundred a day.

SECOMBE.   That's not a cigarette, you nit. That's a ship of the desert.

MILLIGAN.   *(Eccles voice)* I wondered why it tasted funny.

GREENSLADE.   Author's note: no camels were actually harmed in the making of this radio programme.

SECOMBE.   A packet of twenty must be hell to pick up.

MILLIGAN.   *(Eccles voice)* It's catching them when you put the match up to their bottoms that's the problem.

GREENSLADE.   Author's note: no matches were actually harmed in the making of this radio programme.

SELLERS.   *(Bluebottle voice)* 'Ere, my good friend Eccles, can I borrow your camel? I have decided to forsake civilised society and join the French Foreign Legion; which is the Boy Scout movement with guns – and a sneer. So I can be beastly to the Bedouin.

SECOMBE.   Do you speak French?

SELLERS.   *(Bluebottle voice) Au contraire.*

SECOMBE.   How will you make yourself understood?

SELLERS.   *(Bluebottle voice)* Easy, you tickle its hump to turn right or thump its hump to turn left. Tee-hee! *(Sings)* 'Take my hand I'm a stranger in paradise!' Go on, Eccles, you dirty rotten swine, lend me your filthy rotten camel.

Fast forward many years. I am writing on *Friday Night With Wogan* to earn some extra money for my theatre company, writing gags for the co-hosts. Spike Milligan is a guest on the show; thus every technician, cameraman, writer and member of the show crowd into the Green Room at BBC Television Centre to meet the great man.

After the show he arrives at the Green Room door led by an awed and fawning researcher, he glances in at the expecting crowd, shouts: 'fucking freeloaders!' and goes home in a strop...true story.

> **'Everyone moans about the British Raj but we gave India three great things: the railways, the Bible and herpes. You can get shot of the first two but the third one always comes bouncing back'**
> **– Spike Milligan, *Ying Tong*.**

In the play the funniest scene was when Sellers and Secombe turn up at the psychiatric hospital (at least in Milligan's mind) dressed as leprechauns, closely followed by the announcer Wallace Greenslade dressed as a Jewish leprechaun:

Enter SELLERS through the door right on his knees and dressed as a leprechaun. When he speaks it is in an absurd Irish accent.

MILLIGAN.   What kept you?

SELLERS.   Hello there!

MILLIGAN.   What are you?

SELLERS.   Me? I'm a leprechaun. That's a pixie with a shovel.

MILLIGAN.	How are things in Glocca Morra?
SELLERS.	Fucking awful.
MILLIGAN.	To what do I owe this honour?
SELLERS.	I'm your lucky sprite. Every Irishman has one.
MILLIGAN.	My father's Irish but my mother's English.
SELLERS.	Bejesus, what do they do on the anniversary of the Battle of the Boyne?
MILLIGAN.	Beat the living shit out of each other.
SELLERS.	You're half English but only from the waist down, the part that's all bollocks.
MILLIGAN.	What are you doing in a loony bin?
SELLERS.	I could ask you the same question.
MILLIGAN.	Drooling mainly; my father, ever the romantic, once said I was a direct descendant of the Kings of Connaught. What end of kings is this?
SELLERS.	Well – I'm here to bring you luck.
MILLIGAN.	I don't think I'm very lucky at the moment.
SELLERS.	Have you wished upon a shamrock?
MILLIGAN.	Does that help?
SELLERS.	Not at all. Shamrocks? Feckin' useless.

Enter SECOMBE, through the door left, dressed as leprechaun and on his knees. He also speaks in an absurd Irish accent.

SECOMBE.	Hello there!
MILLIGAN.	You're multiplying like rabbits.
SECOMBE.	We're Catholics. We always breed like rabbits.
MILLIGAN.	I'm a Catholic atheist.
SECOMBE.	Do you go to confession?
MILLIGAN.	Yes, but I take a whoopee cushion with me.
SECOMBE.	You've been in England too long.
MILLIGAN.	You're telling me.

SECOMBE. They're a terrible people the English: all bus-queues and buggery.

MILLIGAN. I fought for England.

SELLERS. Not against the poor soddin' Irish I hope?

MILLIGAN. In World War II; you must remember it: it was the only war Vera Lynn did the soundtrack to.

SELLERS. Ah, we didn't have a World War II in Ireland, Milligan. We just had an 'emergency.'

MILLIGAN. What was the emergency?

SELLERS. We ran out of Guinness.

SELLERS and SECOMBE cackle.

MILLIGAN. Aren't you just racial stereotypes masquerading as wacky dwarves?

SECOMBE. To be sure we are.

SELLERS. And top of the morning for mentioning it.

SECOMBE. We'll be gnawing on a potato any minute now.

SELLERS. But aren't we just critters from your imagination, Milligan?

SECOMBE. Not here at all, at all.

MILLIGAN. True. The Home Office says I have to re-apply for citizenship, you see; as I was born outside of the United Kingdom. Despite the fact I fought a war for them for five long years.

SELLERS. The Anglo-Saxon swine!

MILLIGAN. Precisely. I'm thinking of applying for an Irish passport. Which is why I'm seeing you I suppose.

SECOMBE. Ah, we're awful short of people, Milligan. They keep pissing off to America, to be policemen. You'd be welcome.

SELLERS. Mind you, you'll have to explain what you were doing in the British bleedin' Army, you-redcoat-you.

MILLIGAN. I applied for the Irish Navy but the dingy was full.

SELLERS. Ah, a sneer at the paddies again. But what did the English ever do for you, Milligan? Save treat you like dole fodder or cannon fodder?

MILLIGAN. *(Cockney accent)* They made a lovely cup of tea.

SELLERS. You don't know what you are, Milligan: neither Irish nor Indian nor English. No wonder you're sick.

SECOMBE. 'A man without a country is a man without a soul.'

MILLIGAN. Who said that?

SECOMBE. I did.

MILLIGAN. Can you give me some luck? I'm in need of some – fast.

SECOMBE. Of course we can. What with Cromwell –

SELLERS. The potato famine –

SECOMBE. The civil war –

SELLERS. The Black & Tans –

SECOMBE. The rain –

SELLERS. And eight hundred years of oppression –

SELLERS & SECOMBE. *(Together)* Haven't the Irish been blessed to death with luck?

MILLIGAN. *(Laughs)* Did you hear about the Irish mosquito? It caught malaria.

SELLERS. *(Sour)* Why are Irish jokes so simple? So the stupid bleedin' English can understand 'em.

Enter GREENSLADE on his knees and dressed as a leprechaun but wearing a Jewish skullcap. He speaks in an East End Jewish accent.

GREENSLADE. Shalom there! Can you direct me to the Israeli midget convention?

SELLERS. By Jeezus! It's Benny O'Cohen!

MILLIGAN. A Jewish leprechaun, now I've seen everything.

GREENSLADE. So I'm Jewish-Irish. I go to confession but I take a lawyer with me.

MILLIGAN.   That joke was old when Max Bygraves started telling it – in 1847.

GREENSLADE. Oi vey! At these prices he wants originality? What a Meshughe!

MILLIGAN.   My God: it's another racially insulting stereotype.

GREENSLADE. Who's circumcised, me or you?

MILLIGAN.   I didn't want to be circumcised.

GREENSLADE. What happened?

MILLIGAN.   I was walking through Tel Aviv when I was attacked by a deranged rabbi with a blunt penknife.

GREENSLADE. So that's why you walk like a Shikseh.

MILLIGAN.   *(Worried)* I do?

GREENSLADE. Don't worry: you're still one of us.

MILLIGAN.   I am? I thought I was English.

SECOMBE.   Irish.

SELLERS.   *(Indian accent)* Indian, it's so confusing.

GREENSLADE. Do you get indigestion when you eat pickled herring?

MILLIGAN.   Every time.

GREENSLADE. Then you must be Jewish.

SELLERS.   *(Looks off)* Wait a minute: there's a rainbow over Neasden. That pot of gold at the rainbow's end has my name written on it. Last one to a shovel is a big girl's Protestant.

SELLERS exits on his knees. SECOMBE give chase.

SECOMBE.   *(As he exits)* Come back here, you mercenary midget. Don't leave without me.

SECOMBE exits after SELLERS. GREENSLADE remains.

GREENSLADE. What's the matter? Don't you like money? You should be busy writing those God-awful scripts the Goyim find so funny.

MILLIGAN.   I can't.

GREENSLADE. Why not?

MILLIGAN.   I keep getting interrupted by Jewish leprechauns.

GREENSLADE.   You've an excuse for everything you, haven't you, boy?

MILLIGAN.   I care too much for my scripts to churn them out.

GREENSLADE.   It's just gibberish, man.

MILLIGAN.   Yes, but it's my gibberish. There'll never be gibberish like it again.

GREENSLADE.   Oi! What a Nudnick! I'm off. Up the 29 counties!

MILLIGAN.   I thought it was 32 counties?

GREENSLADE.   To you: 27 counties! I can get it for you wholesale!

GREENSLADE exits. A silence; he sighs.

MILLIGAN.   They're right: Irish, English and Indian? I sound like a racist joke. *(Depressed)* Maybe that's all I am: a racist joke.

Milligan was very bitter in later life that the Pythons had stolen his style but open-ended sketches should belong to the world not just Spike. I always thought he missed Sellers and Secombe doing his television shows and radio was really his forte; though his *Q* series did have brilliant bits midst the insanity/dross. Let him be remembered as the surreal master of sound.

But to the Seventies, *The Two Ronnies*, masturbation, the Three Day Week and depression...

The Teenage Years

'Insanity doesn't run in my family, it practically gallops'
– Cary Grant, *Arsenic & Old Lace*.

In a moment of unusual working-class sentimentality my father decided to return to the North-East in 1974. It was quite a surreal experience. We went from watching *Whatever Happened To The Likely Lads* one minute to living on the set the next.

My brother compared leaving West London to live in Gateshead as moving from Shangri-La to Vietnam, during the latter's minor skirmish with the American Military Complex. Despite having Geordie ancestors as far back as Olaf The Camp, last of the rampaging Viking hordes (he didn't pillage, he shopped...) the locals immediately snapped into action and hated the ground I walked on because of my cockney accent. I immediately snapped into action and never left the house.

'Gateshead...where rain goes to cry' – Anon.

But it wasn't as grim as it sounds, it was worse. The great thing about being trapped indoors in the mid-Seventies was that it was an astonishing age for comedy shows. And, boy, I watched 'em all. *The Likely Lads* hasn't aged well, the story of two young jack-the-lads, growing up in Newcastle in the mid-Sixties, but the sequel *Whatever Happened To The Likely Lads,* which returns years later to see the same characters dealing with impending middle age, has remained surprisingly strong, mainly due to the effortless comic acting of James Bolam.

BOB: These streets are ugly, but they have a kind of beauty.

TERRY: Working-class sentiment is the indulgence of working people created through football and rock-and-roll or people like you who moved out to the Elm Lodge housing estate at the earliest opportunity.

BOB: Well I didn't want my kids growing up in these streets.

– The Likely Lads

I got friendly with James when he did a workshop at The National of my farce *Roberto Calvi Is Alive & Well* and, sometime later, we did a TV show called *The Last Postman* which was filmed in Bournemouth. We did a pub crawl through Bournemouth, just the two of us, which got him so pissed I was barred from taking him out again! But we talked about his career and he never wanted to return to the *Likely Lads* as he felt, rightly, it had typecast him to a degree.

Having people shout 'Terry!' at you in the street for twenty five years must be a tad grinding. As Ian Lavender from *Dad's Army* has found with 'Don't tell him Pike!' and John Cleese has found with lorry drivers shouting: 'Give us your silly walk mate!' forty years after the Ministry of Silly Walks had taken its last steps.

James directed my play *Sick Dictators*, about General Pinochet of Chile's arrest (excellently) after that and the only row we ever had was when we were debating a point and I said: 'I'm arguing with a comic genius, what would I know?' And he said: 'ever call me a genius again I'll kick your head in...' They can't take praise these people from Sunderland. He was astonishing in the Twenties drama *When The Boat Comes In* and he's still on top of his game and on top of the ratings in the BBC cop show *New Tricks* as I write this.

'Somebody's stolen the strawberry cream
from the chocolate box called life'
– Bob Ferris, *The Likely Lads*.

Speaking of getting stuck in a role: talk about Warren Mitchell as Alf Garnett. Though anyone who ever saw his astonishing Willy Loman in The National's production of *Death Of A Salesman* would dispute that.

Til Death Do Us Part was a massive hit when it was first screened in the Sixties and was still going strong in the Seventies. As Warren Mitchell seemed to get trapped with Alf so Johnny Speight, the writer, got caught up in his creation to the point he would not write anything else.

In the States it was renamed *All In The Family* and captured the same cultural zeitgeist (check out the episode when the racist Archie Bunker is visited and bested by Sammy Davis Junior come to retrieve a suitcase, it's a blast).

My problem with *Til Death Us Do Part* is that though the actor playing Alf was a Jewish liberal in real life and was being heavily ironic, the audience that was attracted to the show didn't always know that. I've had Indian friends tell me that when they were growing up in Leicester all the words they were being taunted with by the merry little bigots in the playground where learnt from Alf Garnett. There was no irony midst the sneers and hatred.

So it doesn't have a fond place in my heart though the comic acting of Mitchell, Tony 'Stupid Scouse Git' Booth as the son-in-law, Una Stubbs as the daughter and Dandy 'Silly Moo' Nichols was nothing short of excellent.

But we come to the show that saved my life. I was remiss in talking about *Whatever Happened To The Likely Lads* without mentioning the writers: they were Dick Clement and Ian La Frenais and in the creation of *Porridge* they created one of the great comedy shows of my lifetime.

'This prison has a very strong criminal element'
 – Norman Stanley Fletcher, *Porridge*.

Every once in a while a show comes along that is so perfect in script and execution you can't think of one element of the show that could actually be improved. This was the case with *Porridge*, a show set in a Northern prison that ran from 1974-1977. Remarkably it only ran for twenty episodes in all but each was a minor classic of its own.

> **MEDICAL OFFICER: Suffer from any illness?**
>
> **FLETCHER: (Trying to avoid prison-issue shoes) Bad feet.**
>
> **MEDICAL OFFICER: Paid a recent visit to a doctor or hospital?**
>
> **FLETCHER: Only with my bad feet.**
>
> **MEDICAL OFFICER: Are you now or have you at any time been a practicing homosexual?**
>
> **FLETCHER: What, with these feet? Who'd have me?**
>
> *– Porridge*

Fletcher was played with sarcastic cockney cheek by Ronnie Barker, a legendary sketch performer who'd come to fame via *The Frost Report* and *The Two Ronnies* but who showed hidden depths as an actor in the role of a lifetime. Fletcher was a veteran of the prison system who played that system and the rules like a con man.

Prison and cell newcomer Lenny Godber was played by the moon-cheeked and endearing Richard Beckinsale, a youthful veteran of Jack Rosenthal's dating sitcom *The Lovers* and ITV's *Rising Damp*. Beckinsale's early death at twenty-nine always gives the touching scenes between Barker and him an added piquancy. For in every episode there was always a serious moment, a reminder that these men were imprisoned, and that every night a key would turn and they would be trapped in their tiny cell once more.

> **GODBER: I'm only in here due to tragic circumstances.**
> **FLETCH: Which were?**
> **GODBER: I got caught.**
>
> *– Porridge*

The authoritarian head guard was played with imperious authority by veteran Scots actor Fulton Mackay (later adored by a generation of schoolchildren for his performance in Jim Henson's *Fraggle Rock*) whose weekly confrontations with Ronnie Barker were a masterclass in comic acting.

> **MR. MACKAY: I suppose, Fletcher, your wife's told your children you're on a five year safari...**
> **FLETCH: No, she's told them I'm doing missionary work in Scotland.**
> *– Porridge*

Add Brian Wilde's beautiful turn as Mr. Barrowclough – every prison's hand-wringing liberal – and an astonishing performance in several episodes of David Jason as ancient lag 'Blanco' and you have one of the greatest British sitcoms of all time.

It even, by necessity of its time slot, introduced new swear words to the English language: 'naff off' instead of 'fuck off', 'scrote' instead of 'wanker' (?) and 'nerk' instead of 'Berkshire Hunt'. We used them at school with surprising abandon and didn't get told off by our teachers. Absolutely bloody marvellous...!

> *To idle medical student Alan:*
> **'The only thing you study is your navel – you even shave lying down'**
> **– Rigsby, *Rising Damp*.**

Speaking of marvellous, and when one speaks of ITV comedy shows one doesn't say that often (medical sitcom *Only When I Laugh* being the rare exception), one comes to the aforementioned *Rising Damp*.

If anyone is going to run Ronnie Barker close for best comic actor in a sitcom in the Seventies look no further than Leonard Rossiter.

Showing Alan the view from his room:
There's nothing between this house and the Urals. You're breathing the same air as the Tartars, I should charge you extra
– Rigsby, *Rising Damp*.

Leonard Rossiter was already a hugely respected character actor when he came to the role of seedy landlord Rigsby. He was brilliant as the undertaker Mr. Shadrack in the Sixties movie classic *Billy Liar* where he uttered the immortal line: 'I don't want to spoil your weekend, Fisher, so we'll discuss criminal proceedings on Monday.' He was also memorable as the undertaker in the movie musical *Oliver!* and was a revelation playing Brecht in the West End.

He was to go on to be astonishing in *The Fall & Rise Of Reginald Perrin* but for me and many of my generation he will always be the sexually frustrated Little Englander Rigsby, with the cat called Vienna.

His playing against Richard Beckingsale as idle student Alan, Phillip Warrington as posh black tenant Phillip and ethereal (and highly respected stage actress in real life) Frances De La Tour as Miss Jones was a constant delight.

The early death of Richard Beckinsale again taking the shine off the show; a disappointing film followed the fourth and last series.

Shouts at Alan for putting a Labour Party banner on Vienna:
That cat's Conservative! At least, he is during the day
– Rigsby, *Rising Damp*.

There are other influential shows of my teenage years I should mention if I had the time and indeed the inclination (all worth checking out on DVD if you're either unemployed and/or obsessive): *Rutland Weekend Television, Taxi, Rhoda, Fawlty Towers, M.A.S.H, Barney Miller, Dad's Army, Not The Nine O'Clock News, The Odd Couple, Only When I Laugh, Soap, Some Mothers*

Do 'Ave 'Em, I Didn't Know You Cared and *WKRP In Cincinnati* to name but a glorious few...

But to the overwhelming comedic influence of the Seventies: (even if the show started in '69) *Monty Python's Flying Circus*. The influence of the Monty Python team on British culture in those days was not just immense but almost over-powering. Every school playground had some bore droning out bits from their routines. It was, without doubt, the most important comedy show of my formative years.

What *was* their genius? John Cleese and Michael Palin are probably the best sketch performers of all time (with Eric Idle very close behind) and the writing of Palin and Terry Jones, Cleese and Graham Chapman (when he showed up) and Eric Idle has seldom been equalled. Throw in Terry Gilliam's astonishing animation and you have the greatest ensemble of comic talents ever. Though the *Beyond The Fringe* team (Peter Cook, Dudley Moore, Alan Bennett & Jonathan Miller) and *The Goons* ran them damn close. I'll return to the *Beyond The Fringe* team later in the book.

Meanwhile here is my parody (just for the hell of it) of the infamous parrot sketch from my play *Pythonesque*:

> *PALIN stands behind a counter looking very working class and shifty;*
> *CLEESE enters in a raincoat and cloth cap carrying a (huge) stuffed*
> *budgerigar in a cage. He approaches the counter.*

CLEESE.	Is this the shop I bought this very budgerigar from not thirty minutes ago?
PALIN.	Might be, I suppose you want a refund?
CLEESE.	On the contrary, I'm returning to this shop to congratulate you.
PALIN.	Congratulate me?
CLEESE.	This is without doubt the finest budgerigar I have ever owned. It can speak five languages, including Hindustani, tap dance, play piano to concert-hall level, sing the *Hallelujah Chorus*, sometimes in Latin, and complete the *Times* crossword in less

than seven minutes. It's the best pet I've had in thirty-five years of bestriding this island earth.

PALIN. Yeah, but it looks a bit peaky, better give you a refund.

CLEESE. It is not peaky.

PALIN. Yes, it is, it looks all clapped out.

CLEESE. It's just sung the *Hallelujah Chorus* in Latin whilst tap-dancing. You'd be clapped out, mate.

PALIN. Its feathers look all mouldy, and it's gone green look.

CLEESE. It's a green budgerigar, what colour is it supposed to look like? It's not an iguana, changing its colour on a whim every two bleeding minutes.

PALIN. And its droppings are all discoloured.

CLEESE. Your droppings are probably discoloured, there's no dignity in droppings my good man.

PALIN. Nah, it's at death's door, better give you a refund.

CLEESE. I don't want a refund.

PALIN. I could swap it?

CLEESE. Where are you going to find another budgerigar that can play the *Brandenburg Concerto* on the ivories whilst translating Noël Coward motifs into Hindustani? It's not going to happen, my good man.

PALIN. But it's poorly –

CLEESE. This budgerigar is not poorly. It is in the pink, full of vim and vigour, downright perky, hunky dory, in tip top condition, filled with the joys of spring, if it were Irish it'd be on top of the morning; this budgerigar could pass a physical for the S.A.S., it's so healthy it's applied to join a gym, it's one hundred percent, A1, feeling groovy; to conclude it's the fittest budgerigar east of Java, north of the equator and south of the Pecos.

PALIN. Go on, let me buy it back.

CLEESE. Why do you want it back?

PALIN.   I miss him. Well, he's my common law wife.

CLEESE.   Common law wife?

PALIN.   We would have got married but those bigoted swine in the Anglican Church wouldn't let us have the religious ceremony. They say it's in the Bible: 'man shall not lie down with a budgerigar and be fruitful.'

CLEESE.   Then why'd you sell him to me not half an hour ago?

PALIN.   We had a row about his crackers. He said some pretty hurtful things in Hindustani; I responded with some unsavoury comments in Latin, but it was the heat of the moment, we're in love.

CLEESE.   This budgie doesn't know you from Adam.

PALIN.   Yes, it does. Look, he just blew me a kiss.

CLEESE.   No, he didn't.

PALIN.   Well, he winked.

CLEESE.   You liar.

PALIN.   Pouted then.

CLEESE.   Budgerigars do not pout. How can you pout with a beak?

PALIN.   When you're in love anything is possible.

CLEESE.   Wait a minute, how is doing a pastiche of their most famous sketch progressing the story of the Monty Python team?

PALIN.   It's reverential.

CLEESE.   Reverential is all very well but we've been here before haven't we? They're right when they say: 'repetition is the mother of desperation.'

PALIN.   Who says that then?

CLEESE.   Whoever said it first.

PALIN.   But you said 'they' like you knew them.

CLEESE.   I don't know everyone called 'they'. That would be an infinite number of people.

PALIN.   But by the very suggestion 'they say' would be the inference that you actually knew who 'they' were.

FUNNY PEOPLE

CLEESE.   No it wouldn't.

PALIN.   Yes it would.

CLEESE.   Now you're playing Devil's Advocate, just to take up a contrary
             position.

PALIN.   No I'm not.

CLEESE.   Yes you are.

PALIN.   I'm making a perfectly valid point about the absurd
             conversational overuse of the expression 'they.'

CLEESE.   This is ridiculous; this is supposed to be a parody of the parrot
             sketch.

PALIN.   No it's not.

CLEESE.   Yes it is.

PALIN.   It's not.

CLEESE.   It is.

PALIN.   On the contrary.

CLEESE.   I can prove it.

PALIN.   No you can't.

CLEESE.   What am I doing with this budgerigar then?

    This throws PALIN for a moment then:

PALIN.   You might have secreted that budgerigar about your person
             to reveal at a precise conversational moment merely to win
             the right to utter 'they say' whenever the occasion demands it
             without the intellectual validity of its actual usage.

    CLEESE stares, a long pause.

CLEESE.   Say that again.

PALIN.   I would if I could but I can't.

CLEESE.   That's the end of the sketch is it?

PALIN.   Looks like it.

CLEESE.   Righto.

CLEESE begins to shuffle offstage with the budgerigar looking embarrassed. The budgerigar begins to sing: 'The Hallelujah Chorus' enthusiastically.

CLEESE.   *(Hisses)* Not now, not now.

You occasionally hear dissenting voices, perhaps because the Pythons have become almost *too* popular, that they were Never As Good As People Said. Eh...dream on. *Life Of Brian* and *The Holy Grail* are two of the greatest comedy films ever made and probably *the* funniest British comedy films. I'll return to cinema later but if you hear some Comedy Bore claiming the Monty Python team were overrated feel free to yell: 'You do better mook...!' in their faces.

'What's a mook?'
'A mook is a mook is a mook is a mook...' – *Mean Streets*.

Terry Gilliam came to the opening of my play about the Goons and was wildly charming and I literally couldn't speak. It was like meeting a very scruffy...God.

Though they don't come into the era of the Seventies I feel compelled to mention again the only comedy group to almost equal the Pythons in collective genius and that's the *Beyond The Fringe* team.

I was given a record of the London show when I was fifteen or so by one of my mates' Dad who knew I was obsessed with comics and it blew me out of the water. It ran from 1960-1964, starting off at the Edinburgh Festival, transferring to London's West End where it ran and ran and ran before transferring to and conquering Broadway from 1962-1964.

The *Beyond The Fringe* team were vitally important in the history of postwar British comedy. Peter Cook was a great comic turn as E.L. Wisty in later years and always enjoyable in his Pete & Dud and Derek & Clive personas but it was in *Beyond The Fringe* that he conquered if not the world then at least, Cambridge University, London and America.

He always seemed vaguely bored in later life only stirring himself for occasional contributions to *Private Eye* and snide cracks about Dudley Moore's club foot but in the first flush of youth he was like a comet.

Dudley Moore's later life as illness and wasting disease left him unable to even play his beloved piano reads like a Greek Tragedy but in *Beyond The Fringe* he was like a gleeful imp (and offstage according to Jonathan Miller 'an amorous faun' such was his success with women) .

A hugely underrated comic actor he could make audiences laugh as easily with his music pastiches on piano as his one-legged actor auditioning for the role of Tarzan…

Here's my pastiche of Peter Cook's style and the 'Tarzan Sketch' from my play *Good Evening* where Dudley Moore auditions in front of a movie producer for the part of the drunk in the movie *Arthur*:

> *PETER COOK as the movie producer, DUDLEY MOORE enters hopping enthusiastically on one leg and grinning like a loon. He hops through the following scene:*

COOK.   Mr. Moore is it?

MOORE.   That's right.

COOK.   And you'd be here about the role in *Arthur*?

MOORE.   That would be the one, yes.

COOK.   Playing the millionaire drunk?

MOORE.   Yes, the millionaire drunk. Who gets between the moon and New York City. I know it's crazy but it's true.

COOK.   Who gets to grope Liza Minnelli?

MOORE.   That's Liza with a 'z' not Liza with an 's' 'cause Liza with an 's' spells 'Lisa.'

COOK.   Can I be brutally frank, Mr. Moore?

MOORE.   Call me Dudley.

COOK.   Can I be brutally frank, Dudley?

MOORE.   Frank away, frank away.

COOK.   When I, a film producer, advertised in *Variety* for someone to play the role of millionaire drunk, Arthur, I was assuming – call me Mr. Insensitive – that the person auditioning for the role would actually have two legs.

MOORE.   Rather than the one?

COOK.   Rather than the one; not that it's not a nice leg as one leg goes but for the pithy and acerbic exchanges between Arthur and his butler played by John Gielgud I was assuming that the actor in question would not be hopping the whole time because, by and large, it might just get in the way.

MOORE.   John Gielgud having two legs?

COOK.   Precisely. Imagine if you will John Gielgud playing Hamlet with one leg. Hopping up and down Elsinore whilst wringing his hands with Freudian guilt and telling Ophelia to get herself to a nunnery. It wouldn't have the same effect would it? It's very difficult to get black tights from Marks & Spencer's with only one leg for a start. And I suspect Laertes might win the sword fight by hacking at the one leg with his sword, thus making the denouement of the play meaningless.

MOORE.   So John Gielgud will be playing the butler in *Arthur* with two legs rather than one?

COOK.   We considered using only one leg, the other producers and I. For a whole three seconds we considered that. But in our defence, and this will be good because we don't actually have one, we were on artificial substances at the time. Thus in our sobriety we decided John should tackle the role with both feet firmly planted on the ground. We're old fashioned that way.

MOORE.   So what are you saying?

COOK.   To cut to the chase, and if we did have a chase, you only having one leg, I would catch you – we've decided to have an Arthur playing opposite one of the great thespians of our times with two legs instead of the regular one.

MOORE.   So that would mean I don't have a chance of the role?

COOK.   Let's not say that. Let's just say that if any of the 'A' list actors
               we've asked to meet turn up en masse with less than one leg
               between them the role will be yours.

MOORE.   Well, that's something to cling on to.

COOK.   I'd consider clinging on to a crutch first.

MOORE.   Hey-ho, must dash. They're casting *Treasure Island* just down
               the hall.

COOK.   Thank you for coming in.

MOORE.   No, thank you.

COOK.   Feel free not to call us when we don't call you.

MOORE exits singing and hopping:

MOORE.   *(Sings)* Fifteen men on a dead man's chest with a yo-ho-ho and
               a bottle of rum.

Jonathan Miller's comic talents seem to have been lost in the mists of time but watching old recordings of the show it's amazing how strong a comic performer he was. After so many years as a somewhat over-articulate and verbose theatre and opera director his performing origins are unfairly overlooked and to suggest he was the least funny of the group is patently ridiculous.

Thus we come to the glorious Mr. Bennett. Alan Bennett has gone on from *Beyond The Fringe* to become 'A National Treasure' we are told. A description that appals him, thank God, and makes me want to throw up. He's not a National Treasure but he's the best comic playwright since Joe Orton and up there with Wilde and Coward. Of his contempories only Ackbourne and Stoppard can come near him.

Yet he continues to be the most amusing and down-to-earth of men. Any documentary where he revisits the Leeds of his youth is often heart-renderingly touching (about the lonely death of his mother) and wildly amusing. There is a literary giant hiding behind those NHS specs and somewhat unfortunate coloured braces.

I wrote this parody of his style and famous Vicar monologue from *Beyond The Fringe* to cover the death of Peter Cook:

> BENNETT *stands in a pulpit in a vicar's dog collar and addresses the Audience, as a somewhat blithe man of the cloth:*

BENNETT.   I've been asked today, at this memorial service, to say a few words about the late, departed Peter Cook. Despite the fact I didn't know him very well. Despite the fact I didn't know him at all. Despite the fact, indeed, I didn't know him from Adam. Though I suspect Adam would be the more recognisable; ambling down the High Street, as might be his wont, naked as the day he was born save for the fig leaf pinned artfully to his genitalia. But church is no place for words like genitalia. In fact it's beginning to become clear to me that genitalia have no place in church – or indeed life – at all. Though where would we be without them? Some women, I believe, have no need of them. And those women are called lesbians. But I seem to be wandering down a conversational cul-de-sac of my own making. Back to Peter; who was Peter? What lay behind the real Peter's comedic mask? Well, as someone who never met him or indeed liked him, who am I to say? Am I my brother's keeper the Bible often asks; as I have no brother I could not possibly answer that. I have a sister. But, once more, we return to the rather unnecessary subject of lesbianism. And I'd rather ignore all that, as my sister would, if only she didn't have the unnatural urges. Back to Peter; I often think life is like a tin of pilchards. We are always losing the key. Peter found the key to comedy but not the pilchards. If only he had found the pilchards. Might he have been happier? Might he have drunk less? That all depends, I expect, on whether he liked pilchards. And if I mention pilchards again I think I'll scream. Back to Peter; one thinks of Lazarus being raised from the dead. One thinks of Paul on the road to Damascus. One thinks of Lot's wife being

turned into a pillar of salt. One has to think of these things.
One is a vicar. But what, you are perfectly entitled to say,
has all this to do with Peter? Very little indeed; he leaves
behind him three wives, two daughters and Dudley Moore,
the latter a man who once made fun of Moses. God curse
his heathen soul but the Church of England is not one
to bear grudges. Though I'm sure St. Peter will be at the
gates of heaven come Judgment Day, in his Doctor Marten
boots, waiting to hand the little swine a good kicking.
For, yay, mine if a vengeful God, who has a beard, a stern
countenance and is a dead ringer for Gregory Peck; but
let us end with a pointless quote from the Bible followed
by a meaningless hymn. Why? It's the Church of England
way. 'And the Lord said to Abraham: leave this land of fruit
and bounty, journey to the arid deserts of Sinai and there
dwell for a generation in misery and want. Why must we
starve lord? Was it something we said? Asked Abraham in his
bafflement; because I said so sayeth the lord;' And doesn't that
sum up life? You're buggered if you do: you're buggered if you
don't. But church is no place for words like buggered. Though,
by and large, the Church of England is. Let us all sing then,
with hearty insincerity, the hymn: *The Lord Is My Leopard.*

Beyond The Fringe's greatest accomplishment was dragging revue
and theatre comedy away from cheesy/camp musical revue and cheery/
emotionally simple University graduates in boating blazers doing dreadful
songs about punting down the Cam.

I knew little of this when, alongside my Goons and Python records I
played the *Beyond The Fringe* show relentlessly. Here's Peter Cook in *Good
Evening* discussing his own death in the guise of E.L. Wisty:

COOK.   I was minding my own business, pretending to be a
            Norwegian herring fisherman, watching the telly – it was

international drag racing from Latvia, fascinating television at four o' clock in the morning – when there was a knock at the door. I opened it to find a figure in a hooded cloak and scythe. Funny, I thought, I didn't know Jehovah Witnesses came 'round at this time of night. 'Who are you?' I said. 'If you're selling subscriptions for the *Readers Digest* I'm your man. 'Cause, generally, I'm short of toilet roll.' 'I'm Death,' he says. 'You're deaf?' I said. 'So am I,' and slammed the door in his face. He knocked again. I opened the door. 'Hello again,' I said. 'I'm not deaf,' he said. 'Congratulations,' I said and slammed the door in his face. He knocked again. Persistent blighters these nuisance callers; I opened the door. 'You don't seem to understand,' he says. 'I'm not deaf – I'm Death. And I've come to take your soul.' 'I can't give you my soul now,' I said. 'It's international drag racing on the television. The next race is vital. It's Kurdistan versus Armenia for the Asia Minor Cup. Could you wait?' 'I can wait forever for a cup of tea in return,' said Death. 'Frankly I'm gasping.' 'You would be gasping,' I said. 'You're Death. You can have the tea though – but no dunking. I disapprove of dunking. It's a filthy proletarian habit that's led to Britain's moral and social decline.' 'Dunking's not an option,' he said. 'In that case you can come in,' I said. Death took a seat. We watched the drag-racing. Armenia cruised it, as was suspected. 'Is anything else on?' he said. 'I haven't watched television since Albert Tatlock passed away on *Coronation Street*,' showing greater knowledge of popular culture than your average High Court judge. So we watched the highlights of Mongolian Tiddlywinks, ant wrestling from the Congo and the chicken bobsleigh team doing their utmost in the Unusual Winter Games from Guatemala. 'Well, it's that time,' he said when it had finished. 'Time for what?' I said. 'This,' he said, and scythed me down with his farming implement. So I joined the legions of the great departed. Which I thought was a bit rough considering I'd made him three cups of tea and fed him all the digestives he couldn't dunk. But that's grim reaping for you: you just can't get the staff. The obituaries were very moving, of course. They said I was a genius. I never wanted to be a genius. I just wanted never to be bored. But I was. That's life I suppose or the bloody opposite in this case.

But enough of Oxbridge smart-arses and Goon educational simpletons; onwards and downwards: to the comics that influenced me to become an inept yet inane stand-up comic; or as I like to remember my act, a drunk in charge of a microphone...

British Comics

Speaking of my act, here's one of my favourite bits, just for the hell of it:

SMILES. Imagine if you will the story of Jesus as told by the Hollywood studios in the Forties. Humphrey Bogart naturally plays the son of God. *(Bogart voice)* 'The problems of two people don't amount to a hill of beans in this crazy mixed up world but whatever happens we'll always have – Jerusalem!'
Judas is played by Mickey Mouse: *(Mickey Mouse voice)* 'There he is! Washing that woman's feet! Get him Pluto!' Mary Magdalene is played by Marlene Dietrich: *(Dietrich impression)* 'See what the boys in the Temple will have and tell them that I'll have the same!' St. Peter is played by Jimmy Stewart: *(Stewart voice)* 'Every time a bell rings another angel gets its wings. At'ta boy Clarence! I'm looking for Harvey. He stands about yay high!' Pontius Pilot is played by Alfred Hitchcock: *(Alfred Hitchcock voice)* 'Good evening, tonight I'd like to talk to you about murder! *(Sings)* Feed the birds...' Barabbas is played by Kirk Douglas: *(Douglas voice)* 'Stop calling me Spartacus. Why is it every film I'm in I have a tense, nervous headache? Vikings, Schmikings! ' The Good Thief is played by Cary Grant. *(Grant voice, arms outstretched)* 'My name is Leach, Archibald Leach, get me down from here – there's been a terrible misunderstanding. These nails are tearing at my skin and somebody's stolen my cufflinks.' The Bad Thief is played by Burt Lancaster: *(Lancaster voice, laugh and arms outstretched)* 'Crucifixion? Hell, it can only kill ya!' And the Centurion, of course, is played by John Wayne. The Duke:

(John Wayne voice) 'Truly this man is the son of God.' The director of the movie is going: *(Director voice)* 'Loved what you were doing with the scene, John, but could you try and do the line with a little more – awe?' *(John Wayne voice)* 'I surely can, Pilgrim – awe, truly this man is the son of God!'

As you can see doing Cary Grant impressions in the Eighties does suggest how un-topical I actually was.

My double act Smiles & Kemp was equally out of touch with all things fashionable. We did a rather nice pastiche of stiff-upper-lip movies like *Brief Encounter* which I enclose as an example of the sort of material that drove me out of the comedy world and into playwriting as quickly as possible:

(Trevor Howard and Celia Johnson tones)

SMILES.	We can't meet again, he said, clenching his buttocks.
KEMP.	We can't? She stifles a sob. Why ever not?
SMILES.	Because, dramatic pause, I'm emigrating to Kenya.
KEMP.	She grips her hanky feebly. Not – Kenya.
SMILES.	To wear a pith helmet and be beastly to the natives.
KEMP.	She avoids his eyes. It must be terribly, terribly hot in Kenya.
SMILES.	The emotion catches in his throat. It'll be hell, without you.
KEMP.	Don't say it.
SMILES.	I must. He grabs her hand like a cad on steroids. I love you.
KEMP.	You said it.
SMILES.	I said I'd say it and so said it.
KEMP.	If only you hadn't said you'd say it and didn't say it instead.
SMILES.	His loins stir. Under these clothes beats the heart of a passionate man.
KEMP.	Don't say that either.
SMILES.	I've said it and I'll go further. Under these clothes is underwear and under that underwear is a penis that throbs for you.
KEMP.	You're a Naughty, Naughty Nigel, what are you?

SMILES.	A Naughty, Naughty Nigel.
KEMP.	If only you weren't going to Kenya.
SMILES.	If only…
KEMP.	Here's my train coming through the tunnel, time for some obvious phallic symbolism.
SMILES & KEMP.	*(Together)* The End.

Back to comedians of a British bent: the comic I *wish* I'd always seen was Max Miller. If you hear his shows from Finsbury Park Empire from 1939 (and you can get them on BBC tapes) he's so smutty it's gleeful:

> **'Mary had a little bear to which she was so kind**
> **I often see her bear in front...**
> **I'll get on to the next joke here.**
> **Jack & Jill went up the hill just like cock linnets**
> **Jill came down with half a crown**
> **She was only up there two...'ere!'**
>
> **– Max Miller**

To have seen Max even in the latter days of the music halls must have been a sight to behold; overdressed and garish like a colour-blind Victorian pimp. He didn't have one catchphrase, he had a legion: 'Now there's a funny thing,' 'There'll never be another,' 'It's all clean stuff, no rubbish!' 'I don't care what I say, do I?' 'You can't help liking him!'

Because he was a brash (not to say camp) cockney he never worked north of Birmingham, which is no surprise. But he knocked 'em dead in the south and he's certainly the best British comic of his particular generation.

> **'You can lead a horse to water but a pencil must be lead.'**
> **– Tommy Trinder.**

The other big London comic of those times, Tommy Trinder, hasn't aged so well. Orson Welles, during one of his many exiles in Britain, took a violent dislike to Trinder's smug/confident style and oft heckled him apparently; which led to the following exchange during a charity show:

> **TRINDER:** *(On stage)* **Trinder's the name, there'll never be another.**
> **WELLES:** *(Heckling)* **Why don't you change it then?**
> **TRINDER: Was that a proposal of marriage?**

Max Miller was so incensed by Trinder copying his style and stealing his jokes he once saw him sitting in the front row of one of his shows and heckled him from the stage:

> **MILLER: Are you getting all this down?**
> **TRINDER: Can you speak a bit slower?**

Trinder became an increasing anachronism with the progress of the Sixties, managed to lose his gig compering *Sunday Night At The London Palladium* by his loathing of Bernard Delfont, fell from grace with the gods and became chairman of Fulham Football Club instead, the poor wretch.

Bruce Forsythe, who took over from Trinder, I wouldn't call a comic at all. Being a game-show host and 'all-round entertainer'; not that I'm knocking it and there's none better, frankly, at the craft.

I went to see a Christmas episode of *The Generation Game* as a child and the cameras had some sort of technical breakdown. For the next forty minutes Forsythe worked the crowd like a Trojan; swapping banter, insulting the people in the top row, mocking the camera crew and the producer. It was mesmerising.

Again he's one of those performers you wished you'd seen live at the height of his game. He's still doing gags (getting lamer but 'cause its Brucie you don't mind) into his late seventies and that takes some doing. Never does race jokes, never puts anyone down, for someone of his generation that's a fine thing.

Ken Dodd does so long on stage hecklers beg him to stop making them laugh. When he did a stint at the Hackney Empire in the mid-Eighties the Alternative Comedy crowd went down en masse to cynically see the passing of an Old Legend and he tore the place apart. He must have been in his Sixties and he was still going past the three-hour mark.

His only problem in life was with the taxman. Storing half a million pounds under your bed claiming you were saving it 'cause you thought there was going to be an English Civil War is no way to endear yourself to Her Majesties Tax Inspectors methinks; but, again, a benign comedic mind never shitting on those around him.

Dodd was once on a Granada TV show with The Beatles (who he was very friendly with) in 1963 and was bantering that:

> **DODD: I want to start my own band; but I need a name, you know, something earthy...**
> **GEORGE HARRISON:** *(Deadpan)* **How about sod?**
> **DODD:** *(Corpsing)* **I beg your pudding?**

While we're on The Beatles they had a joker of their own of the first rank:

> **AMERICAN INTERVIEWER: What's more important to *The Beatles*? The atom bomb or dandruff?**
> **RINGO STARR: The atom bomb...we've had dandruff.**

Though John Lennon was no slacker when it came to a quip:

> **AMERICAN INTERVIEWER: Is Ringo the best drummer in the world?**
> **JOHN LENNON: He's not even the best drummer in *The Beatles*...**

But do you want to mess with George Harrison?

> **AMERICAN INTERVIEWER: What do you call that haircut?**
> **GEORGE HARRISON: Fred.**

Or McCartney now you think of it:

> **AMERICAN INTERVIEWER: Were you worried about the**
> **oversized rough-necks who were trying to infiltrate the airport**
> **crowd on your arrival?**
> **PAUL McCARTNEY: Eh – that was us.**

Peter Cook and Dudley Moore I have mentioned in their previous incarnation as part of the revue *Beyond The Fringe*. But Pete & Dud were a totally different influence altogether.

In their BBC show *Not Only But Also* they played two philosophising pseudo-cockney morons in Macintoshes holding forth on life.

The BBC, in their infinite wisdom, erased most of their shows whilst keeping every episode of *One Man & His Dog* ever. But, as a kid, I loved 'em. Cook took the inspiration for the two characters from Dudley's Dagenham council estate upbringing and transformed it into surrealist exchanges.

Here, in *Good Evening*, I have Jonathan Miller describe their appeal:

MILLER.　　When *Beyond The Fringe* closed in America I went back
　　　　　　to medicine at first though I eventually succumbed to the
　　　　　　temptation to direct theatre and opera and that was that.
　　　　　　Alan returned to his history but soon began writing the plays
　　　　　　that made him justifiably famous. Dudley, meanwhile, was
　　　　　　asked by the BBC to star in his own show. It was Dudley who
　　　　　　insisted Peter came on board. They'd always, I think, been the
　　　　　　other's preferred performing partner in our quartet. Pete &
　　　　　　Dud were born on that first show. It soon led to the first series
　　　　　　and three brilliant series in all. Why were they so well suited? I
　　　　　　think because Peter gave Dudley his surreal vision of the world
　　　　　　and words. Dudley, meanwhile, gave Peter humanity and a

working class, Dagenhamesque base for his spirals of comic invention. Can I get away with 'Dagenhamesque'? Possibly not but with a head start, the wind behind me, the chance of a black cab and perhaps roller-skates I believe I can make it to the nearest railway station before this audience catches up with me.

Then I cut to 'Pete & Dud' in a pub commenting on his above statement:

COOK and MOORE sit at a table in black Macintoshes wearing cloth caps and black Macintoshes, now in their famous Pete & Dud personae.

MOORE.	Here, Pete?
COOK.	Yes, Dud?
MOORE.	You hear about that Jonathan Miller, the lanky Oxbridge satirist?
COOK.	What about him, Dud?
MOORE.	He was on stage the other night, in front of a paying, civilised audience, well, semi-civilised anyway, and he used the word: 'Dagenhamesque.'
COOK.	The foul mouthed, dirty git, Dud, would he kiss his mother with a mouth like that?
MOORE.	No – but I would.
COOK.	I know but you'd kiss anything. All that education and he talks like he comes from the gutter, or Swindon, which is worse. You can't go 'round bandying the 'D' word to all and sundry. Well, maybe all but never sundry. He'll be using the 'C' word next.
MOORE.	What's that, Pete?
COOK.	'Croydoneese.'
MOORE.	Keep your voice down, Pete. There's a barmaid over there. You know the unwritten rule: no swearing in front of a lady.
COOK.	Who wrote the unwritten rules do you suppose, Dud?
MOORE.	That'd be Moses, Pete. God told Moses the unwritten rules then Moses snapped into action, grabbed a chisel and tablet of stone and didn't write down a bloody thing.

COOK.   I never read that in the Bible, Dud.

MOORE.   You have to read between the lines, Pete. He's a doctor, you know.

COOK.   Who is? God? Which Bible have you been reading, Dud? Did it have the word: 'Zhivago' on the cover? I've got news for you, Dud. That's not the Bible at all, that's the book 'Doctor Zhivago' by Boris Pasternak. About some bloke who gets swept up in the Russian Revolution whilst snogging Julie Christie in the Urals: the animal.

MOORE.   No, I mean Jonathan Miller's a doctor.

COOK.   Oh, right. I could have been a doctor myself of course, Dud. But I never had the Latin.

MOORE.   'Quo Vadis?'

COOK.   You're starting to talk as dirty as Jonathan Miller, Dud.

MOORE.   No, it's Latin, Pete. It means 'where the bleedin' 'ell are you going?' My Dad used to say that to me all the time, when I was peddling off on my push-bike for my organ practice down the local church.

COOK.   Whose organ were you practising on?

MOORE.   The vicar's.

COOK.   That's not legal is it, practising on a vicar's organ.

MOORE.   Let's not walk down Double Entendre Valley, Pete. We'll be here all night. Yeah, 'Quo Vadis?' that's what my Dad used to shout.

COOK.   Why did he shout in Latin?

MOORE.   Your guess is as good as mine, Pete. I used to just shout back: 'Status Quo.'

COOK.   What's that mean?

MOORE.   No idea. But it shut him up.

COOK.   What a strange family you had, Dud.

MOORE.   Still got 'em, Pete: Mum, Dad, Auntie Gertie –

COOK.   A right dirty old cow your Aunty Gertie.

Enter MILLER, looking around him. He is only in MOORE's eye-line.

MOORE. Don't look over there, Pete. You'll never believe who's over there.

COOK. How will I know without looking, Dud?

MOORE. Guess. Go on, guess. You'll never guess who it is in a million years.

COOK. Danny Blanchflower, former midfield dynamo for the mighty Hotspur?

MOORE. Not even warm, Pete.

COOK. Ida Lupino? Gabby Hayes? Jimmy Clitheroe? Gert Frobe? King Zog? C.P. Snow? The Singing Nun? Pinky & Perky? Zeus? Your dirty Aunty Gertie?

MOORE. No, it's Jonathan Miller, that lanky if foul-mouthed satirist.

COOK. *(Looks)* Is it indeed; I want a word with him, Dud. *(Calls)* Here – mate.

MILLER. Are you addressing me?

MOORE. Now he's an envelope, Pete.

COOK. Are you Jonathan Miller, leading lanky satirist?

MILLER. I'm vaguely aware the press might describe me thus, yes; though I would have to be slightly appalled by the description.

COOK. I want a word with you, young man.

MILLER. 'Young'? Bless you.

MOORE. You haven't even sneezed and he's having a go. You tell him, Pete.

COOK. I will, Dud. *(To Miller)* I've heard you've been using the 'D' word to all and sundry.

MILLER. I'm so sorry – I'm not quite with you.

COOK. You might be able to use all the language you like on the West End stage, mate, but you're in the East End now.

MILLER.   Yes, I realise that. I've just been to a football match, to see West Ham. Fascinating, Bobby Moore's sideburns seemed to move of their own accord.

MOORE.   Now he's turning on Saint Bobby of England, Pete, Patron Saint of Fair Play.

COOK.   We're not having it, Dud. Bobby Moore may indeed look as if he's got two live badgers strapped to his cheeks –

MOORE 'corpses'.

COOK.   Don't laugh, Dud. This is a serious matter. *(To Miller)* Let me tell you, Mr. Satire. You can swear all you like midst the Sodom & Gomorrah that is the West End but in this part of the world we're not having any of your gutter talk. There's barmaids present and it's the unwritten rule, as laid down by God for Moses not to write down, that you don't use profane language in front of a lady.

MILLER.   'God'?

COOK.   It's the opposite of 'dog' but means something entirely different. A two-legged hairy apparition over a four-legged one.

MILLER.   A heavenly entity, an all-knowing creator?

MOORE.   The very same.

MILLER.   Poppycock.

MOORE.   *(Tuts)* 'P' word, Pete.

COOK.   What do they teach them at these Oxbridge Universities, Dud?

MILLER.   Where is this mythical 'Oxbridge' I wonder?

COOK.   East of Java. Don't toy with us – Dud got a certificate for Geography.

MILLER.   Perish the thought. I'm sorry but I find the idea of civilised people in this, the second half of the 20th century, believing in some bearded, white, mythical being as the creator of all things simply absurd.

MOORE.   He's trying to blind us with words, Pete.

COOK.   He's succeeding, Dud. I can't see a bloody thing here.

MILLER.   You don't subscribe to the big bang theory?

MOORE.   Now he's getting smutty, Pete.

MILLER.   The big bang theory is that out of the random collision of matter worlds, planets and suns were made.

COOK.   Are you telling me you think that the world of mountains and rivers, trees and oceans was made by nothing other than natural gas? As provided by the Gas Board of eternal existence?

MILLER.   Simplistically?

COOK.   It's my level and I'm sticking to it.

MILLER.   Well – yes.

MOORE.   Isn't that blasphemy, Pete?

COOK.   Yes, it is, Dud.

MILLER.   How can I be blasphemous when I don't believe in God?

COOK.   Now's he trying to throw us with rationality; this is the East End, mate. We haven't had rationality for years.

MOORE.   Well, we had it once but the Kray twins nicked it.

MILLER.   Well, this has all been quite amusing in a vaguely meet-the-proletariat and pull your hair out kind of way but I have to meet some –

COOK.   Did you hear what he called us, Dud?

MOORE.   The 'p' word, Pete. He must have been dragged up.

MILLER.   My father was an eminent Jewish psychiatrist of some renown actually. I don't think he 'dragged' anything in his life.

COOK.   You a Jew then?

MILLER.   Well, Jewish; which is C of E without the hymns or Easter bunny.

COOK.   No wonder you don't believe in God.

MILLER.   Far be it from me to get involved as a pronounced agnostic but you should read up more on the Jewish faith. I think they

	throw a God in there somewhere, except he's less of a mother's boy than Christ.
MOORE.	Why was Christ a mother's boy then, smart-arse?
MILLER.	Well, he did live with her until he was thirty.
MOORE.	Now he's saying Jesus was gay, Pete.
COOK.	Actually he did hang about with twelve other blokes in sandals, Dud. As well as snogging Judas.
MILLER.	You don't have to wear sandals to be gay, surely?
COOK.	Yes, you do. It's the unwritten rule.

Les Dawson was by far and away the best of the bow-tie crowd that came out of the clubs in the Sixties. Though never on *The Comedians* ('just my jokes were' – L. Dawson) he sprang to fame through *Opportunity Knocks* and such Saturday night stalwarts as *The Shirley Bassey Show*.

'In awe I watched the waxing moon ride across the zenith of the heavens like an ambered chariot towards the ebon void of infinite space wherein the tethered belts of Jupiter and Mars hang forever festooned in their orbital majesty. And as I looked at all this I thought... I must put a roof on this lavatory' – Les Dawson.

The late Sixties and early Seventies were an appalling time for subject matter amongst comics: it was all thick Paddy gags and 'Paki' gags. Dawson seemed to be on another planet with his poverty and misery shtick.

With a face like a collapsed prune he used to moan about his childhood, wife and mother-in-law with endearing mock-despair:

'Good evening, ladies and gentlemen – there, that's my first joke. Thank you for that brief spatter of applause that greeted my appearance on the stage of this renovated fish crate. What you are about to see is an act that has given a whole new meaning to the word 'Crap.' I'm not saying my act is bad but the night variety died they held my script for questioning. I don't do this for a living, oh no – just for the luxuries in life – bread and

shoes; I'm so far behind with the rent that arrears are ticked off in the Doomsday Book. Ah, where would we be without laughter? Here.'
– Les Dawson.

(Willie Rushton did a nice variant of that joke: 'Where would we be without laughter? Germany.')

I always think Les Dawson was the Christ of the Northern Comedy Circuit in comparison to Bernard Manning's Anti-Christ; if that's not a metaphor too far. Manning never gave a toss how he got a laugh. Jokes like: 'Aids? I'm never getting that again,' leave me cold. And for a *Jewish* guy to do the gag: 'Can we have a moment's silence for my father who died at Auschwitz? He was pissed and fell out of the machine-gun tower,' leaves me speechless frankly...

'Doctor, I can't stop singing The Green, Green Grass of Home. '
'That sounds like Tom Jones syndrome'.
'Is it common?'
'It's not unusual.' – Tommy Cooper.

But back to heroes not villains: Tommy Cooper was a joy to watch, no matter how old I got. A supposedly inept magician (who was brilliant at magic) he had a weird style all of his own, wearing a fez for all his performing years:

'I went to the doctor the other day I said it hurts when I do that
(*Opens and closes fist*). He said: 'Well don't do it.' – Tommy Cooper.

He famously died on screen doing a live TV show, collapsing having a heart attack, and they had to pull him through the curtain while people watched it at home. The audience at the theatre thought it was part of the act and laughed uproariously. Comics since have said he'd have wanted to go that way: leaving them laughing and all those clichés. But that was no way for a man who'd brought pleasure to millions to go.

'Cause it's strange, isn't it. You stand in the middle of a library and go 'Aaaaaaagghhhh' and everyone just stares at you. But you do the same thing on an aeroplane, and everyone joins in' – Tommy Cooper.

The Irish comic, Dave Allen, was light years away from any other comedy entertainer in the early Seventies. He was doing routines on religious hypocrisy, the Catholic church and the Irish education system run by the clergy years before any other comic in the UK would touch the subject.

'We spend our lives on the run: we get up by the clock, eat and sleep by the clock, get up again, go to work – and then we retire. And what do they give us? A fucking clock' – Dave Allen.

He'd been very influenced by Lenny Bruce and though he obviously had to tone down the excesses of that style for mainstream TV he was still brilliantly subversive. Monday night was Dave Allen night in our house.

'Am I the Irish comedian with half a finger? No, I'm the Irish comedian with nine and a half fingers' – Dave Allen.

He was enraged by religious zealotry and intolerance to the end. God knows what he would have made of the recent child abuse scandals (and systematic cover-ups of paedophilic priests) that are currently engulfing the Catholic church. He'd have a field day – in between crying.

'I'm an atheist, thank God' – Dave Allen.

Amen to that. But from one genius to another:

Billy Connolly is the best comic ever to come out of the British Isles in my lifetime: I can prove it using slides and pie-charts. Name anyone better. A Glaswegian welder who took to comedy like a fish to water via the folk circuit, he's still angry and enraged by life even in his sixties.

'I'm Catholic: I've got an 'A' level in guilt' – Billy Connolly.

He called his early stand-up days 'chasing the witch' as he used stand-up comedy to expunge a terrible childhood of his mother leaving him at the age of four and suffering sexual abuse. Overcoming a famous drink problem he's become the older statesman of the British comedy scene. They keep trying to knock him off his perch but no one has succeeded yet.

'The great thing about Glasgow is that if there's a nuclear attack it'll look exactly the same afterwards' – Billy Connolly.

He came to national fame oddly through a joke a guy told him in a Glasgow pub; he'd come through the folk clubs as a singer with The Humblebums alongside Gerry Rafferty author of 'Baker Street.' He'd started throwing routines in between the songs and gradually the routines took over. Exit left Gerry Rafferty...

He developed a huge following in Scotland but was considered too Scottish and his accent too Glaswegian for English audiences, but word of his records and talent spread south and eventually *The Parkinson Show* came calling, the premier chat show of the time; he told a joke about a guy who murders and buries his wife but leaves her bum sticking up and when a pal asks him why he leaves the arse showing says: 'I needed somewhere to park my bike.' It was wild and rude for the early Seventies and there were only three channels in the UK in those days so by Monday morning he was famous and never looked back.

And, yes, he did make an effort to lessen the thickness of his Glaswegian accent but not by much; his TV documentary tours of Ireland, Scotland, Australia and New Zealand were brilliantly funny television.

'There are two seasons in Scotland. June and winter' – Billy Connolly.

Seeing the man in the flesh is never disappointing. You get an hour and a half of scatological references and swearing to diploma level, as he rages against the hypocrisies and pettiness of modern society; this man was kissed on the forehead by the Comedy Gods.

'Two Englishmen, two Irishmen, two Scotsmen and two Welshmen are washed ashore on a desert island after a plane crash. After a year the two Scotsmen had started a brewery, the two Welshmen had started a choir, the two Irishmen were still fighting on the beach and the two Englishmen were still waiting to be formally introduced' – Billy Connolly.

While we're on the subject of the Sixties folk scene the other big name to come from it who has somehow been underrated in books on comedy is Jasper Carrott. The Birmingham-born funny man was huge in the Seventies.

'Birmingham City will be in Europe next year, if there's a war' –Jasper Carrott (director of Birmingham City).

His smutty version of 'The Magic Roundabout' which was on the b-side of his novelty hit 'Funky Moped' reached legendary status when it was released and he was a great live act and his records sold by the bucket load; the routine about attempting to kill a mole being a particular fave. Not sure why he still doesn't have a cult status really.

Listening to a speeding police siren at the bedroom window:
'He'll never sell any ice creams going at that speed' – Eric Morecambe.

Was there ever a funnier and more beloved English double act than Morecambe & Wise? I doubt it. Getting twenty-eight million viewers for a Christmas show is never going to be equalled, not in the age of multi-channels anyway. It's cool it won't be actually. Guys as nice as they were should be the most popular.

Aside to Wise, about distinguished actor Frank Finlay: 'Ern, there's a drunk on the stage, don't worry I'll get rid of him' – Eric Morecambe.

Morecambe & Wise met as child performers and were inseparable after that, save during the war when Morecambe ended up down the mines pushing coal trucks, which didn't help his already weak heart. After years in the music halls they got their first break on TV which was a famous failure.

They were slaughtered by the critics. Morecambe kept a cutting of the worst review of that first TV disaster: 'Definition of the week: TV set – the box in which they buried Morecambe and Wise,' in his wallet for the rest of his life; imagine the hurt after all those terrible years on the music hall circuit with drunken, indifferent audiences. No wonder he was always amazed by his success and he and Wise were so joyful about their eventual, long-overdue triumph.

'Boom, zoo, yakety-ta!' – Morecambe & Wise.

After that false start their ATV show *Two Of A Kind* was a big hit (with my favourite of their theme tunes: 'Following You Around') but it was when they moved to the BBC that they went through the roof popularity-wise and became the best-loved double act in British television history.

Their catch-phrases and routines were numerous: 'What do you think of it so far?' 'More tea, Ern', 'Short fat hairy legs', 'You can't see the join', 'The play what I wrote', 'Arsenal!' 'Way-hey!' 'There's no answer to that!' 'Just watch it, that's all!' 'You said that without moving your lips' 'This boy's a fool!' 'Get out of that!'

Their Christmas shows were watched by everyone. Kids, uncles, aunties, fathers: their appeal was across the generations. Unlike almost any other double act you can care to mention (Abbott & Costello, Mike & Bernie Winters, Martin & Lewis) these guys didn't only like each other, they loved one another and that love came across in their performances.

Their first writers Hill & Green gave them standard personae: Wise was slick, Morecambe was gormless; but when they went to the BBC they hooked up with the writer Eddie Braben who blurred those lines and made Morecambe more cynical and Wise the inept playwright/dreamer with delusions. It was a marvellous transformation and it took them into the realms of greatness.

ANDRE PREVIN: You're playing all the wrong notes.
ERIC MORECAMBE: I'm playing all the right notes, but not
necessarily in the right order, I'll give you that sunshine.

In my play *Stand Up* I had two comics, Mal and Tony, who used to be in a double act reunited for the first time in years. It is revealed that Tony slept with Mal's wife which was the reason he broke up the act.

Then Mal says:

MAL.   Eric Morecambe didn't die of a heart attack, you know. He had a stroke and he fell. It was falling that killed him. And Ernie Wise said: 'Eric wouldn't have died if I'd been there.' And when he was asked why he said: 'because he was my partner. I would have caught him, wouldn't I?' I would have caught you, Tony. Every time: I would have caught you.

The day Morecambe died was almost like a day of mourning in Britain and that shows how important he was to the nation's psyche. And Wise was right: if he'd been there when Eric fell, he would have caught him. God bless him.

'In India when a man dies, his widow throws herself on the funeral pyre.
Over here, she says, 'fifty ham baps, Connie – you slice, I butter'
– Victoria Wood.

Victoria Wood is not only a brilliant stand-up comic, she's a brilliant writer too. From humble beginnings, well, singing songs on *That's Life*, she has blossomed into one of the best female stand-up comics this country has ever had (arguably the best? I'm open to debate here, folks, but she's close...) A sort of Northern everywoman she can sell out the biggest venues with ease.

Of tennis player Tim Henman: **'Tim Henman is so anonymous.**
He's like a human form of beige' – Linda Smith.

Speaking of women: Linda Smith was a great, droll stand-up who died way too young, Jo Brand easily the most fearless performer I've ever seen live (she used to swat down hecklers like they were slightly irritating gnats) and Hattie Hayridge a deadpan delight.

If ever there was an heir to Eric Morecambe's genial northern charm that person would be Lee Mack, star of *The Sketch Show* (one of ITV's only decent sketch shows ever) and BBC1's gorgeously gag-laden *Not Going Out*.

**'I'm in a relationship – *(Winks at audience)* – so sorry girls,
it'll have to be your place' – Lee Mack.**

A surprisingly tough stand-up act (he once equated being cockney as like getting cancer) he can sell out the Bloomsbury Theatre with ease. He's getting better with the passing of years and his Eric Morecambe impression, by the by, is out of this world.

Of all the Eighties performers I was ever on the same bill as during my dread stand-up years, Bill Bailey has become the biggest and best.

**'"God save our gracious Queen": why would we invoke a non-specific
deity to bail out these unelected spongers?' – Bill Bailey.**

Originally from Bath this hairy druid of mirth started off as part of the musical double act The Rubber Bishops. After a long apprenticeship and endless Edinburgh Festivals and touring he gradually evolved his style of musical parody with wildly surreal asides.

**'I'm English, and as such I crave disappointment. I actively seek it out'
– Bill Bailey.**

Which is one of the best descriptions of Englishness I have ever heard.
Has there ever been a British comic with such articulation? For example:

**'Three blokes go into a pub. Something happens.
The outcome is hilarious' – Bill Bailey.**

'Three blokes go into a pub. One of them is a little bit stupid, and the whole scene unfolds with a tedious inevitability' – Bill Bailey.

'Three blind mice walk into a pub. But they are unaware of their surroundings, so to derive humour from it would be exploitative' – Bill Bailey.

That's not just comedy, that's poetry. There's an almost novelistic style to his one-liners; he describes Milton Keynes as 'Satan's lay-by' and motorway service stations as 'cathedrals of despair.' And he's not wrong is he?

He also asks irritatingly obvious questions we should have asked ourselves years ago, like: 'who photographs kebabs?' And yelled the words we've all wanted to say: 'Hey, Asda, I ain't gonna be your bitch!' Amen.

He fills huge venues with effortless ease in the UK and he's finally getting attention in the States and it's about time too. Because his parody of song styles (and he's a brilliant musician) – whether it be Led Zeppelin, Pink Floyd or Kraftwerk – is universal.

Keep on, hairy troll, keep on...

Before I move to American comics I must give a big high five to comics I didn't have space to mention: Dylan Moran (finest Irish comic since Dave Allen), Paul Merton (funniest man on Radio 4 via *Just A Minute*), Mark Thomas, Harry Hill, Rob Brydon, Armstrong & Miller and the veritable comedic Zeus of Nineties and Noughties sketch-show comedy: Paul Whitehouse.

American Comics

'Guys if you could blow yourselves: ladies you'd be alone in this room right now, watching an empty stage...' – Bill Hicks.

I am a religious man and I believe in the Holy Trinity: and they are Lenny Bruce, Richard Pryor and Bill Hicks. Amen.

'If the Catholic Church is so much in favour of capital punishment they should stop bitching about Christ getting nailed up' – Lenny Bruce.

To call Lenny Bruce merely a Jewish comic is like calling the Grand Canyon merely a ditch. He was more than that. He was an oracle and truth sayer....who happened to like hookers and heroin.

Mort Sahl, his contempory in the Fifties, pointed out that Bruce stopped being funny when he became a martyr to free speech and taken up by the liberal elite, which is true but his movie parodies and bits are still listenable today whereas Sahl is difficult to listen to (still, any Jewish guy who could say to the director Otto Preminger after sitting through two hours plus of his long-winded movie on the foundation of Israel *Exodus*: 'Let my people go Otto...' can't be all bad).

'My mother-in-law broke up my marriage. My wife came home from work one day and found me in bed with her' – Lenny Bruce.

Bruce's routines have cult status: 'White Collar Drunks', 'The Esther Costello Story' 'The Tribunal' (where overpaid showbiz entertainers like

Sammy Davis Junior have to justify their salaries to a heavenly judge), 'Prison Break/Father Flotski' (a classic mockery of over-butch Burt Lancaster prison movies), 'How To Relax Your Coloured Friends At Parties' (still an uncomfortable routine to listen too), 'Thank You Masked Man' (where the Lone Ranger has sex with Tonto *and* his horse) and 'The Palladium' (where an inept American stand-up comic plays the London Palladium and starts a riot) are brilliant in their conception and delivery. His range of voices and mimickery are almost unequalled. At least until Robin Williams came along.

'Satire is tragedy plus time. You give it enough time, the public, the reviewers will allow you to satirize it. Which is rather ridiculous, when you think about it' – Lenny Bruce.

'The Palladium' is almost twenty minutes long and the finest skit he ever put on record. The detail of a bad comic floundering in front of an English audience is amazing. From the Georgia Gibbs singing act that preceeds the comic's turn: a medley of songs, sung sobbing, in memory of the dead of Dunkirk to Palladium owner's Bernard Delfont's smarmy tones are perfectly caught. He was never as good again.

Of taking drugs: 'I'll die young, but it's like kissing God. – Lenny Bruce.'

He was barred from appearing in the UK for a second time and was deported, the home secretary deeming him to be an 'unwelcome alien' despite the fact his father was British. His first appearance in London at Peter Cook's Establishment Club had inspired a whole generation of British comic performers. Jonathan Miller believed he blew *Beyond The Fringe* out of the water and created a new standard for satire.

In my play *Good Evening*, about the *Beyond The Fringe* team, I have Peter Cook as E.L. Wisty describe bringing Bruce to London:

COOK.   After *Beyond the Fringe* was established I opened the Establishment Club, a club with satirical barbs winging all over the place. Many a night I had to duck to avoid a barb. One nearly took a barmaid's eye out. My biggest coup was bringing the foul-mouthed American comedian Lenny Bruce over to play the club. Nobody had warned me he was a junkie. Well, actually, they had but I thought they'd used the expression: 'flunky', which has quite a different meaning altogether. I just thought he'd be ingratiating and eager to please, without the bloody great needle sticking out of his arm. 'Where's my heroin?' he said reasonably, as soon as his plane touched down. Thus, at four o'clock in the morning, I found myself scouring Soho for narcotics. Though British chemists are notoriously liberal in their handing out of Aspirin, paracetamol or anything else that can help you actively commit suicide on a whim they take a dim view of ladling out heroin at four o'clock in the morning without a prescription. 'What's it for?' they asked. 'A terrible case of haemorrhoids,' I said. Not believing me they sent me back to Lenny Bruce empty-handed. I expected him to unleash a foul-mouthed tirade as he was a notorious foul-mouthed berk but all he said was: 'Alright, I'll have some chocolate cake instead.' It doesn't give you the same high as heroin, chocolate cake apparently, but can be as dangerous. Particularly when injecting it into your arm. Needless to say, this being England, getting chocolate cake at four o'clock in the morning turned out to be more bloody difficult than getting the heroin...

Bruce said the unsayable: about the Mafia, the Church, the Kennedys, the law and there was a price to be paid for that.

**'Because I'm Jewish, a lot of people ask why I killed Christ. What can I say? It was an accident. It was one of those parties that got out of hand...'
– Lenny Bruce.**

Bruce always thought the cops were after him, they called him paranoid, but they were. His attacks on religion, particularly the Catholic Church, in bits like 'Christ & Moses' (where Christ returns to earth and sees the expensive rings on cardinals and the Pope's hands and then notices Hispanic children were dying of curable diseases in the Bronx) and 'Religions Inc' brought the wrath of Cardinal Spellman down on his head, the head of the Catholic Church in America.

'They say if you're attacked by a shark you should beat it away with a nearby object...like what, the stump of your left leg?' – Lenny Bruce.

Spellman and the Chicago police department in particular came after him with a vengeance. At one stage he was busted for saying 'schmuck' by an undercover cop they'd sent along because he spoke Yiddish.

It gave my play on Lenny its title. The cops said the word was obscene when it's actually slang for 'discarded foreskin.'

**'I want to help you if you have a dirty-word problem. There are none'
– Lenny Bruce.**

Lenny became consumed with defending himself against what he saw was an illegal conspiracy to repress his right to free speech. He was right but the comedy still went out of the window as he read transcripts from his trials to an increasingly disinterested audience.

'Lenny Bruce died of an overdose of police' – Phil Spector.

When he died of a morphine overdose, naked next to a toilet bowl, aged just forty, the cops released photos of the scene. If you look at the law men posing next to the body they look almost gleeful that Bruce was dead before his time.

They called Lenny obscene but that's obscene to me.

If Lenny had looked out into the audience in the early Sixties he might have seen a nervous-looking black man sitting, watching and taking notes. The young man had just survived two years of racism in the US Army. His name was Richard Pryor.

Once Richard took to the stage and started talking into a microphone nothing was the same again. For Richard Pryor was not a human being, Richard Pryor was a force of nature, a scorching comet that landed on this planet to observe us for a while before imploding.

'My Daddy died fucking. He came and went at the same time'
– Richard Pryor.

To have a grandmother who ran a brothel, a mother who turned tricks and a father who was a part-time pimp it would seem the gods were telling Richard that life was never going to be easy, and by god it wasn't. Heart attacks, divorces, cocaine addiction, freebase pipe addiction, he did them all. Though attempting to set light to himself after pouring rum over his body in a suicide bid, at the height of his freebasing habit, might have been overdoing the self-destruction a tad.

'I went to Zimbabwe. I know how white people feel in America now,
relaxed! 'Cause when I heard the police car I knew they weren't
coming for me' – Richard Pryor.

The man lived about eight lifetimes. During that time he made several classic films and put out a concert film of two of the best examples of stand-up ever: *Richard Pryor Live* and *Live On Sunset Strip* (*Here & Now,* filmed in New Orleans in front of a curiously hostile audience, has its great moments but is not in the same league).

'Marriage is really tough, because you have to deal with feelings...
and lawyers' – Richard Pryor.

To call *Richard Pryor Live* a work of art might be pushing it but not by much. In the course of an evening Pryor recreates randy monkeys, psychotic guard dogs, his own heart attack, black funeral mourners, Muhammad Ali, John Wayne, startled deer and a deranged stuttering Chinese waiter – and that doesn't get close to how brilliant the mime and the physical expressionism were.

I spoke to black British comic Lenny Henry about it and he said it was the most perfect comedy gig ever put on film. Though *Live On Sunset Strip* where he discusses his suicide attempt by setting light to himself with brutal honesty comes a very, very close second...

> **BART: Are we awake?**
> **JIM: We're not sure. Are we...black?**
> **BART: Yes, we are.**
> **JIM: Then we're awake...but we're very puzzled.**
> **– Blazing Saddles.**

Pryor co-wrote Mel Brooks' *Blazing Saddles* and his humour is all over the piece. Cleavon Little did a fine job in the lead but it would have been fascinating to see Pryor in the role; the studios wouldn't take the risk. For his comic acting check out *Silver Streak* and *Stir Crazy* with Gene Wilder and for dramatic acting check out the amazing *Blue Collar* with Harvey Keitel and Yaphet Kotto or *Lady Sings the Blues*, the story of Billie Holiday, with Diana Ross. The guy could act brilliantly when pushed.

Here's some examples of the great man's wisdom:

> **'I had to stop drinking, 'cause I got tired of waking in my car driving 90.'**

> **'I'm not addicted to cocaine. I just like the way it smells.'**

> **'When that fire hit your ass, it will sober your ass up quick! I saw something, I went, "Well, that's a pretty blue. You know what?**

That looks like fire!" Fire is inspirational. They should use it in the Olympics, because I ran the 100 in 4.3.'

'I'd like to make you laugh for about ten minutes – though I'm gonna be on for an hour.'

'I went to penitentiary one time, not me personally, but me and Gene Wilder went there for a movie. Arizona State Penitentiary, population 90 percent black people. But there are no black people in Arizona. They have to bus motherfuckers in!'

'When I was in Africa, this voice came to me and said, "Richard, what do you see?" I said, "I see all types of people." The voice said, "But do you see any niggers?" I said, "No." It said, "Do you know why? 'Cause there aren't any."'

'There are only two pieces of pussy you're gonna get in your entire life, that's your first and your last.'

'Fuckin' is good for you, Jack. Getting some pussy beats having a war.'

'Freebase? What's free about it?!'

'I believe in the institution of marriage, and I intend to keep trying until I get it right.'

'I went to the White House, met the president. We in trouble.'

On YouTube check out the job interview skit he wrote to do with Chevy Chase. One of the most famous sketches in *Saturday Night Live*'s history. Chase in a word association exchange uses increasingly racist terms and Pryor reacts with comic anger. As memorable now as when it was first broadcast:

CHASE. Spear-chucker.

PRYOR: White trash.

CHASE. Jungle bunny.

PRYOR: Honky.

CHASE. Spade

PRYOR: Honky-honky.

CHASE. Nigger.

PRYOR: <u>Dead</u> honky.

– *Saturday Night Live*

How a man that full of love and life as Richard Pryor could end up wasting away slowly from MS is a question only God can answer.

So we've had the black guy and the Jewish guy so now it's time for the white guy. Bill Hicks never saw the sun so might have been the whitest white guy who ever lived. For a kid from Austin, Texas, he was certainly not Southern tanned.

'But I'll tell you this. Where does this idea that childbirth is a miracle come from. Ha, I missed that fucking meeting, okay? "It's a miracle, childbirth is a miracle." No it's not. No more a miracle than eating food and a turd coming out of your ass. It's a chemical reaction, that's all it fucking is. If, you wanna know what a miracle is: raisin' a kid that doesn't talk in a movie theatre. Okay, there, there, there is a goddam miracle. It's not a miracle if every nine months any yin yang in the world can drop a litter of these mewling cabbages on our planet. And just in case you haven't seen the single mom statistics lately, the miracle is spreading like wild-fire. "Hallelujah!" Trailer parks and council estates all over the world just filling up with little miracles. Thunk, thunk, thunk, like frogs laying eggs. "Thunk, look at all my little miracles, thunk, filling up my trailer like a sardine can. Thunk. You know what would be a real miracle, if I could remember your daddy's name, aargh, thunk. I guess I'll have

to call you Lorry Driver Junior. Thunk. That's all I remember about your daddy was his fuzzy little pot-belly riding on top of me shooting his caffeine ridden semen into my belly to produce my little water-headed miracle baby, urgh. There's your brother, Pizza Delivery Boy Junior'"
– Bill Hicks.

Hicks began performing aged fourteen, sneaking out of the house, to play the burgeoning late Seventies Austin comedy scene. The first time his mother was aware he was doing comedy was when a neighbour stopped her in the street and told her: 'maybe you should look at the way that young man was raised...'

'The human race? We're a virus with shoes' – Bill Hicks.

I have been thunder struck meeting Americans who have never heard of Hicks but it was England and Ireland who elevated Hicks to cult status years before he was famous in the States (mainly for having his monologue censored and cut on *The Letterman Show*).

The albums *Dangerous* and *Relentless* were good enough but the albums he made just before his early death from pancreas cancer: *Rant In E Minor* and *Arizona Bay* lift him to the status of legend (and *Love, Laughter & Truth* is not far behind).

Here's Hicks on the Creationists who believe the world to be only 12,000 years old (by counting back the ages of characters in the Bible):

'You know, the world's 12,000 years old and dinosaurs existed, and existed in that time, you'd think it would have been mentioned in the fucking Bible at some point: 'And O, Jesus and the disciples walked to Nazareth. But the trail was blocked by a giant brontosaurus...with a splinter in his paw. And O, the disciples did run a shriekin': 'What a big fucking lizard, Lord!' But Jesus was unafraid and he took the splinter from the brontosaurus's paw and the big lizard became his friend. And Jesus sent him to Scotland where he lived in a loch for O so many years, inviting

thousands of American tourists to bring their fat, fucking families and their fat dollar bills. And O, Scotland did praise the Lord: 'Thank you Lord, thank you!' – Bill Hicks.

It took a long time for the penny to drop amongst our American cousins that they had a genius in their midst. Sam Kinison, the loud ranter and fellow Comedy Outlaw from the Austin scene, was a lot more popular Stateside, as was the dread Andrew 'Dice' Clay.

You wonder why Hicks was more popular in the UK? Read him in full flow in front of an audience in Pittsburgh, entertaining his fellow countrymen:

'Y'all about to win the election as the worst fucking audience I've ever faced. Ever...ever...ever! S'all right. S'all right. No, listen folks. Here's the deal. I know you're getting concerned. Let me assure you right now – there are dick jokes on the way. Relax, I'm a professional. Here's the deal: I editorialize for forty minutes. The last ten minutes we pull our 'chutes and float down to dick-joke island together, OK? And we will rest our weary heads against the big, purple, thick-vein trunks of dick jokes, and we sit in our comfy beanbag chairs, and giggle away the dawn like good American audiences. OK? Penis jokes are comin' up. Relax. I understand what country I'm in' – Bill Hicks.

His rants against Jay Leno and *The Tonight Show*, George Bush, Creationism, pro-lifers, Iraq, Waco & David Koresh, Jesse Helms, Rush Limbaugh, gays barred from the military, flag burning, legalisation of marijuana, anti-smokers, the LA riots and advertising amongst others, are brilliant.

'I've been travelling a lot lately. I was over in Australia during Easter. It was interesting to note they celebrate Easter the same way we do; commemorating the death and resurrection of Jesus by telling our children a giant bunny rabbit left chocolate eggs in the night. Now, I wonder why we're fucked up as a race. You know, I've read the Bible. I can't find the words 'bunny' or 'chocolate' anywhere in the fucking book. Where do you come up with this shit? Why those two things? Why

not 'Goldfish left Lincoln Logs in your sock drawer'? As long as we're making shit up, go hog wild. At least a goldfish with a Lincoln Log on its back crawling across your floor to your sock drawer has a miraculous connotation to it!' – Bill Hicks.

There is one stunning bit where he compares American foreign policy to Jack Palance's gunman bullying poor farmers in the movie *Shane* which is almost eerie in its perfection, I've certainly never heard a better Jack Palance by the way:

(Makes gunshot sounds) 'Did you see that? He had a gun...' – Bill Hicks.

ANYONE who wants to be a comic, is a comic, was a comic should listen to *Rant In E Minor* and *Arizona Bay* and catch any Hicks footage on YouTube of his English shows (The Dominion gig is well worth a look).

'The world is like a ride in an amusement park, and when you choose to go on it you think it's real because that's how powerful our minds are. The ride goes up and down, around and around, it has thrills and chills, and it's very brightly colored, and it's very loud, and it's fun for a while. Many people have been on the ride a long time, and they begin to wonder, "Hey, is this real, or is this just a ride?" And other people have remembered, and they come back to us and say, "Hey, don't worry; don't be afraid, ever. Because this is just a ride." And we...kill those people. "Shut him up! I've got a lot invested in this ride, shut him up! Look at my furrows of worry, look at my big bank account, and my family. This has to be real." It's just a ride. But we always kill the good guys who try and tell us that, you ever notice that? And let the demons run amok? But it doesn't matter, because it's just a ride. And we can change it any time we want. It's only a choice. No effort, no work, no job, no savings of money. Just a simple choice, right now, between fear and love. The eyes of fear want you to put bigger locks on your doors, buy guns, close yourself off. The eyes of love instead see all of us as one. Here's what we can do to change the world, right now, to a better ride. Take all that money we spend on weapons and defenses

each year and instead spend it feeding and clothing and educating the poor of the world, which it would pay for many times over, not one human being excluded, and we could explore space, together, both inner and outer, forever, in peace' – Bill Hicks.

Alas, he died aged 32 of pancreas cancer and we lost one of the great ones. I have dope-head friends in Wales who believe Bill Hicks died for our sins. I don't think that's true but you can't stop me half-wanting to believe it. The one true comic genius of my generation, gone way too soon, man, that sucks.

Footnote: Denis Leary has had a hard time in the UK because of his 'borrowing' of Hicks' style back in the day (and jogging joke). He has been dismissed as a copycat, which is a shame as *Rescue Me*, his fire service show, which has run for five series now is very, very funny indeed.

'If O.J. wasn't famous, he'd be in jail right now. If O.J. drove a bus, he wouldn't even be O.J. He'd be Orenthal, the bus-driving murderer' – Chris Rock.

If Richard Pryor has a natural successor step forward Chris Rock. The black comic who, like Eddie Murphy before him, came to fame through *Saturday Night Live* (another show they never show on Brit TV, why lord, why?) For an Afro American to go on stage and do a routine entitled 'Niggas vs Black People' takes some doing. Actually it takes balls of clanking steel and it caused huge controversy. But Pryor would be proud of him.

As a child his parents bussed him to an almost all-white school in Bensonhurst, an Italian-American neighbourhood, where he didn't get much of an education but 'had his ass kicked on a regular basis.'

This experience led to the show *Everybody Hates Chris*, set in the Eighties, which he narrates. A great ensemble cast recreate Chris's childhood and school days. It's shown on Channel 5 here and is laugh-out-loud funny.

'You're never going to meet the perfect person. The timing's off. You're married, she's single. You're a Jew, he's Palestinian. One's a Mexican, one's a racoon. One's a black man, one's a black woman. It's always something' – Chris Rock.

I should mention Eddie Murphy who is a startlingly good comedian and in his two Eighties stand-up films *Delirious* and *Raw* proves it. His impersonations of Bill Cosby and Richard Pryor are so accurate as to be near perfection and his send-up of Italian-American machismo is gloriously spot-on. The only thing wrong with him as a comic is the general appalling view of humanity and particularly his misogyny and homophobia. The Aids gags particularly stick in the craw. As Snozzle Durante oft put it: 'you got to have heart.' I never thought Murphy had that as a stand-up. Without the humanity you're just a bigot with a microphone.

Roseanne Barr is a better comic than is given credit. Her show was brilliant during the first four or five seasons before self-indulgence let alone self-destruction took over; she's returned to her comedy roots and gone back to gigging.

'The quickest way to a man's heart is through his chest' – Roseanne.

Whatever you think of her she's the real thing. A Middle-American Jewish mother with weight issues and she's mad as hell about being stereotyped and vilified for what she is. Keep on keeping on.

'What a beautiful day. It's the kind of day that starts with a hearty breakfast and ends with a newsreader saying: "before turning the gun on himself"' – Dan Conner, Roseanne.

George Carlin is not known in the UK. He was such a disciple of Lenny Bruce he got busted at the same time as Bruce (by refusing to show the cops his ID) just to get thrown in the same paddywagon. He began as a middle-of-the-road comic doing standard shtick but had a similar Road To Damascus moment as Richard Pryor during the late Sixties. I believe narcotics were involved.

'The alcohol warning should be more to the point. Warning: alcohol turns you into the same asshole your father was'– George Carlin.

Like Bruce he was obsessed with language and the repression of free speech. His most famous routine: 'Seven Words You Can Never Say On Television': shit, piss, fuck, cunt, cocksucker, motherfucker and tits, is well worth a listen though I'd avoid his appearances in *Bill & Ted's Excellent Adventure* movies.

'I once had a leather jacket that got ruined in the rain. Why does moisture ruin leather? Aren't cows outside a lot of the time? When it's raining, do cows go up to the farmhouse, "Let us in! We're all wearing leather! Open the door! We're going to ruin the whole outfit here!" ' – Jerry Seinfeld.

I've always had time for Jerry Seinfeld, apart from the *Seinfeld* show which I loved (the 'Yadder Yadder' and 'Master Of My Own Domain' episodes are classics by the by). His stand-up is not angry or earth-shatteringly original but he's got a great style to him. A sort of warm, endearing New York cynicism thing going on; some comedians find him lightweight but I'd disagree. Not every comic has to be on the edge of drug-fuelled self-destruction. There'd be a lot higher casualty rate if they were.

'Airline hostesses show you how to use a seat belt in case you haven't been in a car since 1965' – Jerry Seinfeld.

The Button-Down Mind of Bob Newhart was released in 1960 (so popular it knocked *The Sound Of Music* from the top of the Billboard charts and won a Grammy). And though other comics who made albums from that era – Shelley Berman and Mort Sahl – are pretty unlistenable to now Newhart stays as fresh as ever.

The stammering monologues/phone conversational style was as dry and original then as it is now. Everyone knows *The Driving Instructor* monologue but my favourite is *Introducing Tobacco To Civilisation*. Whereby Sir Walter Raleigh rings the incredulous head of the East India Company back in England to expound the joys of tobacco:

'You can shred it up, put it on a piece of paper and roll it up...don't tell me, Walt, you stick it in your ear right, Walt? *(Listens)* Or between your lips? Then what do you do to it, Walt? YOU SET FIRE TO IT?'
– Bob Newhart.

There's also great sketches where Superman is trying to get his leotard back from the dry cleaners and the new janitor at the Empire State Building rings his employer to ask what to do about King Kong climbing the building...

One of the funniest moments of the *Dean Martin Show* on YouTube is where he tries to do the *Returning A Gift* routine (about an embarrassed man returning a 'Mr. Wonderful' toupee that's fallen into the cheese dip at a party) with Dean Martin, who keeps cracking up. 'What I really want is a straight man who'll stop laughing,' ad-libs Newhart which cracks Martin up more. 'You sure you worked with Lewis?' he adds. 'Our stuff was never as funny as this,' quips Martin back; priceless stuff.

Of *the toupee:* 'I know it stays on in a hurricane. You see, I'm from Iowa, we really don't get that many hurricanes. Mainly I just want it to stay on when I go down for the cheese dip' – Bob Newhart.

Martin was such a fan he had Newhart on his show twenty-four times and he made eight appearances on *The Sullivan Show*. He really is a one-off.

'I don't like country music, but I don't mean to denigrate those who do. And for the people who like country music, denigrate means 'put down''
– Bob Newhart.

While we're on the subject of *The Dean Martin Show,* and I do keep coming back to it, one of the most viewed clips from the show on YouTube is the 'Drunken Pilot' sketch. Surprisingly, as Martin did the drunk shtick he's not playing the drunk. That honour goes to Foster Brooks who wanders into an airport bar off his nut and about to fly a plane. Brooks' whole act was a drunk routine and its diction and delivery is a wonder to behold. He also showed up on *Dean Martin Celebrity Roast* and always stole the show.

> **BROOKS: You know, those fluffy things...**
>
> **MARTIN: You mean clouds?**
>
> **BROOKS: You sure you're not a pilot?**
>
> *– Dean Martin Celebrity Roast*

Joan Rivers had a long, long apprenticeship. But she's been at the top for forever now. Lenny Bruce was always a fan and encouraged her, so did Johnny Carson, who promoted her and allowed her to sit in as guest host on many occasions until their Famous Feud. She's a tough old broad with a gloriously bitchy edge who tells it like it is.

'I have no sex appeal. I have to blindfold my vibrator'– Joan Rivers.

Oddly her attacks on celebrities have made her very popular with other celebrities. When she stopped doing jokes about Cher's face lifts and appalling dress sense Cher rang to complain...which is nice.

She's certainly self-depreciating. In my play *Funny Girls* I recreated an event in the late Fifties when a recently divorced twenty-four-year-old Joan Rivers found herself opposite an eighteen-year-old Barbra Streisand playing her lesbian stalker in a dreadful off-Broadway play. Streisand and Rivers discuss their various flaws in the following:

BARBRA.   Jeez, I wish I was a guy.

JOAN.   You do?

BARBRA.   It never seems to matter if male actors have odd shaped faces.
           I'm used to it of course. I've heard all the gags, all my life.
           All the ant-eater jokes: when ants see this nose coming they
           commit hari-kari before it gets to them. All the: with a nose
           like that in Brooklyn you can smell fresh bagels in Canada. Oh,
           I've heard them all: your nose is so big you make Pinocchio
           look like a cat. Is that your nose or are you wearing it in for a
           friend? Is the friend Cyrano de Bergerac? What do you cover
           those nostrils with when you sneeze? Man-hole covers?

           *She goes to the clothes rail and picks up a battered Trilby, puts it on and
           begins to do jokes in a vaudeville tone:*

BARBRA.   To pick a nose like that you need all seven dwarves. With
           a nose like that when you sneeze in Flatbush they get a
           hurricane in Queens. Does W.C. Fields know you've stolen his
           nose? If that nose got any bigger it'd be on Mount Rushmore.
           That nose could bat for the Yankees. With a nose like that who
           needs enemies? Smell the roses? It can inhale the roses. That
           nose could snort more cocaine than Harlem. Those nostrils are
           so deep they found oil. When that nose goes swimming people
           panic, they think it's a shark fin. That nose is so sharp Woody
           Woodpecker is taking it to court for infringement of copyright.
           That nose is so long Pan-AM is using it as a new runway. That
           nose is so vast Columbus discovered it. That nose is so huge
           New York just named it the sixth borough. If that nose is a
           penis it's having an erection –

JOAN.   Enough already, you think you got troubles?

BARBRA.   What have you got to complain about?

JOAN.   Hello, I was wallflower of the year 1948-1953 running. You
           want jokes about yourself? Listen to this –

           JOAN spits out jokes fast as a machine gun:

JOAN.   I'm so ugly the English burn me on Guy Fawkes Night. I'm so
           ugly I was turned down for a job as a gargoyle. I'm so ugly I
           could model for death threats. I'm so ugly I was kicked out of

the Mafia. I'm so ugly I give Ernest Borgnine hope. I'm so ugly Quasimodo wouldn't take me to his prom night. I'm so ugly I have to Trick or Treat by phone. I'm so ugly I make onions cry. I'm so ugly when my parents took me to the zoo the zookeeper said: 'thanks for bringing him back.' I'm so ugly I looked out of the window and got arrested for mooning. I'm so ugly they shot *The Creature from the Black Lagoon* in my shower. I'm so ugly in strip joints they pay me to put my clothes back on. I'm so ugly even Picasso won't draw me. I'm so ugly Churchill wants to use me as his body double. I'm so ugly I was turned down for a wanted poster. I'm so ugly Alsatians won't hump my leg. I'm so ugly Disney based Goofy on me. I'm so ugly NASA want to send me into space instead of the chimp. I'm so ugly when little green aliens land they shout: 'hello neighbour!' I'm so ugly the Ku Klux Klan make me wear a hood even after meetings. I'm so ugly – *(Stops)* nah, I got nothing.

Carol Burnett is another lost treasure to English audiences. She was memorable as the cruel orphanage manager out to do Little Orphan Annie down in the musical *Annie* but for many years she was the sketch queen of American TV with *The Carol Burnett Show*. Ably supported by Tim Conway and Harvey Korman (the enthusiastically hammy villain from *Blazing Saddles*). There is a great famous corpsing clip on YouTube as Tim Conway tries to talk about a midget and an elephant and Burnett and the rest of the cast lose the plot completely. Burnett did a famous skit on the Civil War where she had her Scarlett O'Hara wear an entire curtain rail. It inspired my Civil War skit from my Thirties vaudeville piece *Backstage*:

The stage of a New York theatre, 1939, HANNA and HERB LEIBMAN are performing their famous 'Civil War' skit: Hanna dressed as a Southern Belle, Herb as a Confederate officer.

They both speak in highly exaggerated Southern accents:

HANNA.   Oh Beauregard, Beauregard, must you leave so soon?

HERB.   I must, Beulah.

HANNA.   But the magnolias are in bloom and you're still bow-legged from your last horse ride.

HERB.   I was bow-legged before my last horse ride, Beulah.

HANNA.   Yes, but skilled surgeons can put that right, Beauregard. Stay, until the magnolias fade, wither and begin to stink of armpit.

HERB.   I must leave, Beulah, for the Yankees march on Richmond.

HANNA.   Oh Richmond, Richmond, flower of the South, must even Richmond fall? I can still see it now, in all its vanished glory: the mansions, the malaria, the bigoted drunks grovelling in their own filth –

HERB.   Yes, it's a rat-infested slum but it's our rat-infested slum, Beulah. The Yankees will never have it – unless they use violence of course.

HANNA.   Has General Lee got a fiendish plan?

HERB.   Yes, to retreat and retreat some more, then surrender begging for mercy. He's brilliantly fiendish that way.

HANNA.   Oh fiddly-dee! Is the South we knew really gone forever, Beauregard, the fried chicken, the grits, the flatulence?

HERB.   It's gone with the wind, Beulah.

HANNA.   I've said it before for no reason and I'll say it again: fiddly-dee!

HERB.   (Bitter) I blame that carpetbagger and cur: Abraham Lincoln.

HANNA.   (Aside) I hear he's Jewish.

HERB.   (Aside) I heard that too.

HANNA.   (Aside) Do you think it's the beard?

HERB.   (Aside) That or the hat.

HANNA.   (Louder) All the South ever wanted was to do revolting things with chewing tobacco in between keeping people in chains. Why couldn't the North leave us be?

HERB.   They don't understand tradition, Beulah. Why up North they let anyone vote, even midgets.

HANNA.   Them New Yorkers is ignoramuses I tells ya.

HERB.	Wise words. *(Beat)* Oh Beulah, if I fight the Yankees and lose a leg, to a cannon ball say, will you still love me?
HANNA.	No, but it will mean I can thrash you at table tennis.
HERB.	Curses, it's been catastrophe and despair since Gettysburg.
HANNA.	True, nowadays I can't even get gingham anywhere.
HERB.	*(Appalled)* No gingham? Say it ain't say, Beulah, say it ain't so.
HANNA.	It's so; why, in the old days you could pluck gingham from these trees. My Daddy grew gingham on this very plantation. He built it from a swamp and when the price of gingham fell he turned it back into a swamp again, and sold mosquitoes to gullible tourists. *(Wistful)* Happy days of yore.
HERB.	*(Frowns)* Yore what?
HANNA.	Yore guess is as good as mine.
HERB.	Now's not the time for puns, Beulah.
HANNA.	*(Mock surprise)* It's *not*?
HERB.	Not when the slaves are revolting.
HANNA.	You're telling me. You'd think with the money we're paying them they could afford soap.
HERB.	We don't pay them, Beulah, that's why they're called 'slaves'.
HANNA.	I wondered why they were so surly. Why only yesterday, before they left, one of them inserted a banjo up my ass.
HERB.	They're bitter that way.
HANNA.	The banjo still works; don't get me wrong, but every time I tune it my eyes water.
HERB.	Who will fetch the gingham crop, Beulah, now your slaves are gone?
HANNA.	You mean – they're not coming back?
HERB.	The Yankees have freed them, Beulah.
HANNA.	You mean – I'll actually have to actually pay the help?
HERB.	That's why we've been fighting so nobly these last four years, Beulah, nobly fighting so other men have to do all the work while we sit on our fat Southern asses sipping mint julep.

HANNA.	The South will have our revenge, Beauregard.
HERB.	How Beulah?
HANNA.	Four tedious hours of *Gone With The Wind* has brought many a good man down.
HERB.	Do I look like Clarke Gable, Beulah?
HANNA.	Only if you were to wear a hood over your head, Beauregard.
HERB.	I can't wear a white hood until after the Civil War, Beulah.
HANNA.	With your face I'll start knitting one now.
HERB.	The angels in heaven broke the mould when they made you, Beulah. Now I must ride my trusty steed, Rebel, to Richmond and destiny.
HANNA.	The local hillbilly trash ate your trusty steed, Beauregard, remember?
HERB.	*(Mutters)* Those bastards will eat anything. *(Beat)* No wonder I'm so bow-legged. I have to ride an imaginary horse over hill and dale. The dales I don't mind – but the hills are hell.
HANNA.	Adieu, Beauregard, and remember if you do get wounded: even a flesh wound, paper cut or splinter, don't come back.
HERB.	You've a big heart, Beulah, now away, Rebel, away!

HERB exits left, miming he is riding a horse.

HANNA.	Oh Tara! Tara! *(Thinks)* Who the hell is Tara? *(Shakes fist at heavens)* I swear to the heavens above: I shall never eat grits again.

HANNA goes crossed-eyed; there is the sound of a distant fart, a snap blackout.

'Republicans have called for a National African-American Museum. The plan is being held up by finding a location that isn't in their neighbourhood' – Conan O'Brien.

I love Conan O'Brien, I think he's one of the funniest guys in America, can I watch him in the UK? Can I hell. For two reasons: none of the UK channels show his show and NBC just hung him out to dry and brought back Jay 'The Chin' Leno to *The Tonight Show*.

He was a writer who wrote for *The Simpsons* who was plucked from the backroom to run a late, late night chat show. Then he took over the Letterman slot when Letterman went to CBS.

'Starbucks says they are going to start putting religious quotes on cups. The very first one will say, 'Jesus! This cup is expensive!"
– Conan O'Brien.

A funny Irish-American satirist with a wild, zany streak; I wish he was known in the UK more.

'Today the LA Times accused Arnold Schwarzenegger of groping six women. I'm telling you this guy is presidential material'
– David Letterman.

The son of an Indianapolis florist and former weatherman, stand-up comic David Letterman has been doing a late-night chat show since 1982. Taking the slot after *The Tonight Show* with Johnny Carson, Letterman was Carson's chosen heir when he retired but NBC had other ideas and installed the bland but safer Jay Leno.

Much to Carson's consternation as he and Letterman had become such great friends that after he retired he contributed jokes to Letterman's monologue on *The Late Show*, which Letterman would signal by doing Johnny's signature golf swing at the end of the gags.

After it was revealed he'd had several affairs with female staffers on his show: **'Things have got so frosty at home that not even my Sat-nav is talking to me' – David Letterman.**

Relentlessly funny over the years Letterman's show is another that somehow was never considered good enough to be shown on British television, though it was shown at 1am on Channel 4 for a while.

I tend to catch up on him via YouTube. His monologues are always great, his rapport with celebrity guests hilarious, his Top Ten Lists (check out the ones from Homer Simpson and Ricky Gervais) are a scream and his glee over Jay Leno coming and going on *The Tonight Show* verges on ecstatic; heartily recommended viewing.

After a critically mauled hosting of the Oscars: 'I had no idea the thing was televised. Boy, is my face red.' – David Letterman.

Steve Martin may act in somewhat cosy family movies these days but my God the man was a great stand-up. In the Seventies his records were like comedic gold. You couldn't get them over here for a long time so to meet someone with a copy and get a tape of it was like winning the comedy Pools.

'For sincere advice and the correct time, call any number at random at 3.00 am.' – Steve Martin.

Martin began his career at Disneyland. He was ten years old. He lived two miles away and got a job selling guidebooks. This guy was committed to a career in show business from an early age. He became mesmerised by Merlin's Magic Shop and within a couple of years was performing tricks behind the counter eight hours a day. It was his schooling. By the time he left at eighteen he'd mastered the banjo, juggling and magic. He played folk clubs and coffee houses in the mid-Sixties before getting his big break writing on *The Smothers Brothers Comedy Hour*. It was *Saturday Night Live* (which he hosted a record fourteen times) that made him a household name.

'First, the doctor gave me the good news: I was going to have a disease named after me' – Steve Martin.

Such was his popularity that by 1977 he was playing amphitheatres and Sports stadiums. He described playing to upwards of fifty thousand people a night as 'beyond scary, like Nuremberg'. The necessary loss of subtlety playing such vast crowds led him to quit while he was ahead and turn to movies. He made *The Jerk* and the rest is history. With *Father Of The Bride II* and the *Sgt. Bilko* movie one wishes one could rewrite history sometimes but please, please, please check him and Bernadette Peters out in the movie version of Dennis Potter's *Pennies from Heaven*, they and the film are sublime.

'I believe that Ronald Reagan can make this country what it once was: an Arctic region covered with ice' – Steve Martin.

A very funny British DJ called Paul Burnett used to have a 'Fun At One' slot every day on his show on Radio One when I was a kid. And it was on this show I first heard Woody Allen and his 'Moose' routine. My life was never the same. I wasn't Jewish but I was nerdy and nebbish so I've spent the rest of my life faking it. I'm a Fake Jew. What can I tell you? I even celebrate Jewish holidays. Or would if I could pronounce them...

'Those that can't do: teach. Those that can't teach: teach gym' – Woody Allen.

With his somewhat scandalous private life and the critical scorn towards his later poorer movies people have forgotten what an astonishing comic this man was. Allen claims he was very influenced by Mort Sahl and though there is a similarity in the hesitant, intellectual style the content is light years apart. Allen's language, one-liners and imagery are miles ahead of Sahl or anyone.

'She was an atheist, I was an agnostic, we couldn't agree on which religion not to bring our children up in' – Woody Allen.

I can name the bits: 'Eggs Benedict', 'The Vodka Ad', 'Down South', 'Kidnapped', 'The Library' and quote vast tracks of his routines: 'I spent that winter in a wheelchair,' 'I removed a thorn from his paw,' 'Sheldon stepped on my dog,' 'My grandfather, on his deathbed, sold me this watch,' 'I tended to place my wife under a pedestal,' 'The Bible would have gone through my heart if it wasn't for that bullet,' 'We were married by a reformed rabbi, a very reformed rabbi, a Nazi,' 'My parents' values were God and carpeting,' 'He'd just learnt to walk erect that morning,' 'I lapsed into that old Navaho trick of screaming and begging for mercy,' 'My parents realise I have been kidnapped, snap into action and rent out my room,' 'An Eskimo who sang *Night & Day* six months at a time,' 'Scott and Zelda Fitzgerald came home from their wild New Year's party – it was April, 'I won two weeks at inter-faith camp where I was sadistically beaten by boys of all colours and creeds.'

I'll come back to his movies in a later chapter but, for a short little schnook from Brooklyn, Allen is and will always be a Comedy Giant.

I was always interested in the way Jewish comedy evolved from the Vaudeville shtick of the Marx Brothers to the jazz-free form stream of consciousness of Lenny Bruce to the nebbish college literate routines of Woody Allen.

In my play *Schmucks* a nerdy comic, Joe Klein, loosely based on Woody meets Lenny Bruce and Groucho Marx during the New York blackout of 1965, as the two Jewish legends vie for Joe's comic soul. In this extract they get Joe to do his (failing) act and then do their versions of how his material should be:

LENNY.   Alright, kid. You want new material, wacky material? Huh?
           Talk about the riots in Watts that left thirty-five dead 'cause
           coloured people couldn't take being beat up and shot to death
           by racist cops anymore. Talk about Pope Paul VI coming to
           New York and calling contraception the devil's work while
           the streets of South America are teeming with starving kids.
           Talk about a hundred and twenty-five thousand troops being
           sent to Vietnam. A country we haven't declared war on yet.
           Talk about Gemini 3 going into space with bright, shiny white
           college graduates aboard while Porto-Rican children are dying
           of curable diseases in the Bronx. Talk about the Rosenbergs;
           how they went to the electric chair with all the major

religions screaming for their blood. 'Cause, after all, the Ten Commandments says: 'Thou Shalt Not Kill – Sometimes.' Talk about the march from Selma to Montgomery, Cassius Clay, venereal disease, Alabama. Talk about anything but how ugly your wife is or your brother-in-law is so dumb; be different, be remarkable, be something.

JOE.   *(Beat)* Could you be a little more – specific?

LENNY.   Christ, kid. Aren't you listening?

JOE.   I'm listening, I'm listening: I'm not understanding but I'm listening.

LENNY.   Show us – show us what you've got.

JOE.   *What?*

LENNY.   You want help, it starts here.

LENNY climbs up on a table, pulls down a hanging lamp, and ties it to a chair, making a spotlight on the wall.

JOE.   What's that?

LENNY.   Your stage: *(Mock pompous English)* The London Palladium. *(Normal voice)* Let's see: you're sharing the bill with Sophie Tucker, The Scottsboro Boys, Ray Charles juggling, a bell-ringing leper *(Mimes a bell being rung by a leper before his arm falls off)* and the I.R.A. singing *When Irish Eyes Are Smiling*. *(Makes a bomb noise, followed by a fey voice)* Knock 'em dead, sweetie. Love from the crowd at Lindy's.

JOE.   I can't do my act here.

LENNY.   Why the hell not?

JOE.   You've already seen my act –

LENNY.   I saw you being heckled.

JOE.   But here, I've no audience.

LENNY.   Face it: it can't get worse than the Bitter End.

JOE.   I know but – hell – of all the cockamamie ideas –

GROUCHO.   Know the secret of comedy, kid?

JOE.	Timing?
GROUCHO.	Nope.
JOE.	Diction?
GROUCHO.	Nope.
JOE.	I give up, what's the secret of comedy?
GROUCHO.	Balls.
JOE.	Hey – I've got balls.
GROUCHO.	You could have fooled me.
JOE.	Alright, God-damn it, alright, you want an act? You got one.

JOE goes into the light. Half-hearted. LENNY stands in front of him doing an Ed Sullivan grimace.

LENNY.   *(Ed Sullivan voice)* Later in the show Bobby Kennedy wrestles Jimmy Hoffa naked – but first a big Sullivan Show hand for that rising young dean of satire: Joe Klein.

LENNY steps aside with a theatrical flourish. JOE unwillingly goes into his act. At no time during the act do LENNY or GROUCHO laugh at his routine, which is poorly delivered.

JOE.   Good evening, ladies and gentlemen. My name is – eh – Joe Klein – and I've just got here from the Village. Greenwich Village that is, Beatnik Central as I like to call it; you can hardly move for the bongos. I live in a cold water apartment. But it's very hygienic. You have to wipe your feet on the drunk before entering the block. You might call it a slum but I can't. If I do my landlord beats me up. He's very strict. He doesn't allow visitors after ten, or before ten. He's a Nazi. I don't mean that he's a nasty, bigoted, fat, vicious person, though he is. I mean he's an actual Nazi. He wears a pointed helmet – to bed. He was the only guy not to surrender at Stalingrad. He still resents the United States sending the Soviet Union wheat. He thinks we should bomb the Soviet Union first – then send the wheat. He's slightly to the right of – John Wayne. On the day of the Kennedy assassination he claims he was only cleaning his rifle on the grassy knoll. John Wayne that is: not my landlord. John Wayne made the film about the Alamo. Which I saw; a movie so long, dull and pompous Mexicans in the back were shouting: 'In the name of God – if it shortens the movie – let them win!' I share my apartment with a folk singer: Kirk. He only wears black. Even his dandruff is black. He's in mourning for Dylan going electric. He got beat up at a peace rally, by Martin Luther King, on the March on Washington, in a struggle for the microphone. King was trying to tell the crowd he had a dream. But Kirk had been smoking marijuana; he insisted on telling the crowd about *Puff The Magic Dragon*. So King socked him in the mouth. Kirk took it well. He joined the Ku Klux Klan. Kirk's girlfriend, Zelda, is a mime artist. She never speaks. It gets in the way of her day job: she's an air traffic controller. And –

JOE stares at LENNY and GROUCHOs sombre faces.

JOE.   Can I stop now? Unsmiling? Your faces turned to rock. It's like playing Mount Rushmore. So the act has a few weak spots –

LENNY and GROUCHO exchange a look.

GROUCHO.   Weak spots? Some guys have a drum roll follow their gags. You have a hearse.

LENNY.   You sound like a thousand other guys, man.

JOE.   I thought you were going to help?

LENNY.   Alright, one: get away from the lame one-liners. Show your personality.

JOE.   I haven't got a personality. My parents wouldn't let me have one.

LENNY.   Two: toughen it up. This is 1965 for Christ's sakes. You don't have to pussy-foot anymore. You're not on the Borscht belt now.

JOE.   I do well on the Borscht belt.

LENNY.   Anyone can do well on the Borscht belt. They laugh to take
                their minds off the food. Three: get angry, there's no anger
                there.

JOE.   I don't want to get angry, I want to get laughs.

LENNY.   Comedy without anger is pointless.

JOE.   Tell that to Martin & Lewis.

LENNY.   I did. Look, I tell you what, I'll do your act, man.

JOE.   You?

LENNY.   Trust me.

*LENNY goes and stands in front of the light. LENNY pretends he is in
mid-act, begins with a JOE impression. Capturing his nervous style:*

LENNY.   My name is Joe Klein. I think I might be Jewish. I'd like to
                apologize in advance for being here. I live in the Village. The
                beatnik's I live with dropped acid last week, fried their brain
                cells, ended up retarded, joined the Young Republicans. I live
                eight floors up. On a clear day you can see Nixon sweating;
                that peace-loving Quaker who wants to bomb the shit out
                of Hanoi, single-handed. My landlord is a Nazi. He's worse
                than a Nazi, he's Hitler. *(German accent)* I wanted to paint but
                those fools in Vienna would not recognize my genius! Walls I
                painted! Ceilings I painted! With a brush! With a roller! Still,
                they said I was untalented! It was easy for Michael and Angelo
                to paint the Sistine Chapel! They gave them a ladder! Me? I
                have to paint ceilings getting piggy backs from Goebbels!'
                (Normal voice) He's slightly further to the right than John
                Wayne. There's a myth that John Wayne only gets an erection
                when someone Vietnamese dies. I think that's bullshit. I think
                he gets an erection every time he hears the *Star Spangled
                Banner*. He wasn't on the grassy knoll. I know who was. I've
                read the Warren Report. It's such a whitewash there's only one
                guy could have been responsible: Warren. Of course, Kennedy
                should never have gone to Texas. He was Catholic. The English
                wear pith helmets to shade from the sun – Texans use white

hoods. When *Ben Hur* was shown in Texas they edited out the Jewish scenes. To this day Lyndon Johnson thinks a three hour Biblical epic is a twelve minute chariot race. The only movie duller than *Ben Hur* is *The Alamo*. Very uplifting, all about Texas's fight for freedom from the tyranny of Mexico; why did they want to leave Mexico? 'Cause Mexico abolished slavery. That's why. *(Bar-room bigot voice)* Those Hispanics are so backward. Didn't they know? Coloured people just loved to pick cotton for nothing. That's why they were singing all the time: 'cause they were so happy. *(Southern black voice)* 'Beat me again, Massa, 'cause I'm having such a great time with this cotton pickin' shit. Long as I can sing *Camptown Races* and tap dance who needs dignity and freedom? What Massa, why am I wiping my ass with the Confederate flag? I thought that was what it was for – '

JOE.　　　　Stop it. That's not funny. Black people have been through hell in this country.

LENNY.　　You're not listening to what's behind the words. *(To JOE)* Can you see what I did? You take Southern racism and you mock it, mock it until it hurts. Make a point, shock the audience; make them laugh at their own bigotry until they're sick.

JOE.　　　　I can't do that kind of thing.

LENNY.　　Why not?

JOE.　　　　Eh – I want them to like me?

LENNY.　　What's liking got anything to do with it?

JOE.　　　　Everything.

GROUCHO.　Let me do his act.

LENNY.　　You, shouldn't you be in a retirement home in Florida?

GROUCHO walks into the spotlight.

GROUCHO.　*(To Lenny)* You want funny, schmendrick? Watch and learn. *(Goes into spiel)* Ladies and gentlemen: my name is Klein – 'Klein every mountain, ford every stream.' But insincerely, folks: it's great to be here. Frankly it was this or a hernia operation. I'd like to talk about home. There's no place like home: unless it's someone else's home. Then it's no home at all – it's away. My mother takes in washing, the neighbours washing and she won't give it back no matter how hard they beg. My father presses pants, while people are still wearing them. He's currently serving a fourteen stretch in San Quentin for attacking strangers with a hot iron. But it's okay: he'll be out for Christmas, which is a shame, we're Jewish. We don't celebrate Christmas. Just think what Santa Klaus would save in reindeer feed if he knew there's no such thing as Christmas. But, you know and I know, there ain't no such thing as a sanity clause. And if I say that again I'll scream. I know who killed Kennedy. It was the Germans, getting him back for going to the Berlin Wall, and saying: *(German accent)* 'Ich bin ein doughnut.' Doughnuts is fighting talk in the Fatherland. *(Beat)* The Alamo, I'm so old I played the Alamo. John Wayne used to be called Marion. He slept with every Robin between here and Sherwood Forest: the minx. Martin Luther King said he had a dream. About black people and white people coming together – and getting the yellow people. They're already doing that in Vietnam. Who said dreams don't come true? Vietnam: the war they only started so Bob Hope could have something to do. Speaking of racial harmony: I had a dream last night about Lena Horne – naked; she had all her clothes on but she still wouldn't sleep with me: the minx. And if I say that again I'll scream. But now a song about a girl whose legs are so bandy they look like the Arc d' Triumph. Only more men have been through them than the Arc d' Triumph. They call her Lydia. Her parents – Mr. and Mrs. Virus – wanted to call her Chlamydia but the rabbi wouldn't go for it, the narrow-minded fool. I sing like Caruso, Robinson Caruso. If you want to join in the chorus – don't – I hate competition.

'Look Pinky, it's Bill Gates, the world's richest nerd'
– Pinky, Pinky & The Brain.

The great thing about having a kid is that you can watch cartoons again without guilt. In the late Nineties there were some great shows. *Pinky & The Brain* concerned two lab mice: one with delusions of world domination and the voice of Orson Welles, the other a complete village idiot with a vaguely English accent.

> **BRAIN: Now, Pinky, if by any chance you are captured during this mission, remember you are Gunther Heindriksen from Appenzell. You moved to Grindelwald to drive the cog train to Murren. Can you repeat that?**
>
> **PINKY: Mmmm, no, Brain, don't think I can.**
>
> *– Pinky & The Brain*

Each week Brain would try and take over the world and each week, the gormless Pinky would somehow screw it up. There was also a hamster nemesis called Snowball floating about. Both myself and my son adored it.

> **PINKY: Egad! You astound me, Brain!**
>
> **BRAIN: That's a simple task, Pinky.**
>
> *– Pinky & The Brain*

There was also *Animaniacs*. A wild Warner Brothers show, created by Steven Spielberg's company, deliberately trying to recreate the anarchy of Tex Avery and Chuck Jones, the Forties originals. Three maniac anarchistic critters (Yakko, Wakko & Dot) caused mayhem on the Warner Brothers lot, having been kept in a water-tower since the Thirties.

> **DOT: Oh, oh, my heart aches with the sorrow of a thousand scouts! No merit badge. I mourn my loss.**
>
> **YAKKO: Say, those acting classes are really paying off!**
>
> *– Animaniacs*

If you stumble across one of the shows on the Cartoon Channel you will be laughing until they take you away.

YAKKO: Alas, poor Yorik!

DOT: *(Translating)* **'Woah! Check out Skull Head'.**

YAKKO: 'I knew him Horatio: A fellow of infinite jest, of most excellent fancy.'

DOT: *(Translating)* **'He was funny.'**

YAKKO: 'He hath borne me on his back a thousand times.'

DOT: *(Translating)* **'He gave me piggy back rides.'**

YAKKO: 'And now, how abhorred in my imagination it is! My gorge rises at it.'

DOT: *(Translating)* **'I'm going to blow chunks.'**

– Animaniacs

I know Homer Simpson is not a real person. He is yellow and has only four fingers on each hand. But he's a lot realer than most people I ever met. Is *The Simpsons* the greatest comedy show of all time? Well, it's damn close, 'bro. Who knew Fox could do something good? Starting off life as a segment at the start and finish of the *Tracey Ullman Show* (a very fine comic performer almost overlooked in her own country which is weird, she's a classy turn) *The Simpsons* has grown into a global phenomenon. There's the mugs, the bathmats, the t-shirt, it's all become too much in a way and the show isn't as good as it once was. But at its peak...my word. The writing and vocal performances are almost unsurpassable. Forty favourite quotes folks:

COMIC BOOK GUY: Your questions have become more redundant and annoying than the last three 'Highlander' movies.

HOMER: Operator, this is an emergency, get me the number for 911!

SIDESHOW BOB: I'll be back. You can't keep the Democrats out of the White House forever, and when they get in, I'm back on the streets, with all my criminal buddies.

LIONEL HUTZ: This is the most blatant case of false advertising since my suit against the movie The NeverEnding Story.

HOMER: I'm normally not a praying man, but if you're up there, please save me, Superman.

CANADIAN RESCUE TEAM TO AMERICAN RESCUE TEAM (competing to save the Simpsons from drowning): Shatner stealing Mexico touchers!

HOMER: You don't like your job, you don't strike. You go in every day and do it really half-assed. That's the American way.

CHIEF WIGGUM: Fat Tony is a cancer on this fair city! He is the cancer and I am the…uh…what cures cancer?

KENT BROCKMAN: The phony pope can be identified by his high top sneakers, and incredibly foul mouth.

HOMER: Kids, you tried your best and you failed miserably. The lesson is, never try.

LIONEL HUTZ: Where did a little girl like you learn such a big word as 'shyster'?

HOMER: When will I learn? The answers to life's problems aren't at the bottom of a bottle, they're on TV!

GRANDPA SIMPSON: Dear Mr. President, There are too many states nowadays. Please, eliminate three. P.S. I am not a crackpot.

TROY McCLURE: Hi. I'm Troy McClure. You may remember me from such self-help tapes as 'Smoke Yourself Thin' and 'Get Some Confidence, Stupid!'

MR. BURNS: I'll keep it short and sweet: Family. Religion. Friendship. These are the three demons you must slay if you wish to succeed in business.

KENT BROCKMAN: And the fluffy kitten played with that ball of string all through the night. On a lighter note, a Kwik-E-Mart clerk was brutally murdered last night.

MR. BURNS: Whoa, slow down there, maestro. There's a 'New' Mexico?

HOMER: *(to Queen Elizabeth II)* But we Americans are England's children! I know we don't call as often as we should, and we aren't as well behaved as our goody-two shoes brother, Canada. Who by the way has never had a girlfriend. *(Whispers)* I'm just sayin'…

KENT BROCKMAN: Earlier in this broadcast, I said a word so vile it should only be uttered by Satan himself while sitting in the toilet. '

KRUSTY THE CLOWN: And this ends Krusty's non-denominational holiday fun fest. So have a Merry Christmas, a Happy Chanukah, a Krazy Kwanzaa, a Tip Top Tet, and a solemn, eventful Ramadan. Now, over to my god, our sponsors.

PBS PLEDGE DRIVE HOST: It's easy to see why it's England's most long-running series – and we're showing all of them, all 7 episodes.

KENT BROCKMAN: Just miles from your doorstep, hundreds of men are given weapons and trained to kill. The government calls it the Army, but a more alarmist name would be… The Killbot Factory.

HOMER: Kids, just because I don't care doesn't mean I'm not listening.

CHIEF WIGGUM: Okay, okay, move along, nothing to see...oh my God, a hideous plane crash! ...keep moving, nothing to see here...

HOMER: *(To BART)* I always knew you had personality. The doctor said it was hyperactivity, but I knew better.

HOMER: Look, all I'm saying is, if these big stars didn't want people going through their garbage and saying they're gay, then they shouldn't have tried to express themselves creatively.

APU: Yes! I am a citizen! Now which way to the welfare office? I'm kidding, I'm kidding. I work, I work.

HOMER: *(After meeting Tony Blair)* Wow, I can't believe we just met Mr. Bean!

MR. BURNS: A lifetime of working with nuclear power has left me with a healthy green glow...and left me as impotent as a Nevada boxing commissioner.

SIDESHOW BOB: Your guilty consciences may make you vote Democratic, but secretly you all yearn for a Republican president to lower taxes, brutalize criminals, and rule you like a king!

PRINCIPAL SKINNER: Fire can be our friend; whether it's toasting marshmallows or raining down on Charlie.

COMIC BOOK GUY: Human contact: the final frontier.

KRUSTY THE CLOWN: And now, in the spirit of the season: start shopping. And for every dollar of Krusty merchandise you buy, I will be nice to a sick kid. For legal purposes, sick kids may include hookers with a cold.

HOMER: How could you?! Haven't you learned anything from that guy who gives those sermons at church? Captain Whatshisname? We live in a society of laws! Why do you think I took you to all those Police Academy movies? For fun? Well, I didn't hear anybody laughing, did you? Except at that guy who made sound effects *(Makes sound effects and laughs)*. Where was I? Oh yeah! Stay out of my booze.

HOMER: Lisa, vampires are make-believe, like elves, gremlins, and Eskimos.

KENT BROCKMAN: *(At the St. Patrick's Day parade)* All this drinking, violence, destruction of property...are these the things that we think of when we think of the Irish?

HOMER: The code of the schoolyard, Marge. The rules that teach a boy to be a man. Let's see, don't tattle, always make fun of those different from you. Never say anything, unless you're sure everyone feels exactly the same way you do.

MR. BURNS: This anonymous clan of slack-jawed troglodytes has cost me the election, and yet if I were to have them killed, I would be the one to go to jail. That's democracy for you.

KRUSTY THE CLOWN: *(To PRESSMEN)* And I maintain that those tourists were decapitated before they entered the Krustyland House of Knives. Next question.

HOMER: *(To MARGE)* You know, I've had a lot of jobs...boxer, mascot, astronaut, imitation Krusty, baby-proofer, trucker, hippie, plow driver, food critic, conceptual artist, grease salesman, carny, mayor, grifter, bodyguard for the mayor, country western manager, garbage commissioner, mountain climber, farmer, inventor, Smithers, Poochie, celebrity assistant, power plant worker, fortune cookie writer, beer baron, Kwik-E-Mart clerk, homophobe and missionary. But protecting Springfield, that gives me the best feeling of all.

Favourite episodes? 'Bart v Australia', 'The Regina Monologues' (set in London) and the 'Marge vs the Monorail' episode with Leonard Nimoy. Laugh? I nearly bought a round.

Speaking of laughter...if you hear a strange bellowing noise coming from my house sometime in the afternoon it will be me watching the reruns of the US comedy improvisation show *Whose Line Is It Anyway*.

The Canadian Colin Mochrie and the American Ryan Stiles were imported to the UK for the English show and were a huge hit, despite the wildly over-smug Clive Anderson being host of the show.

In the States Drew Carey is the host and Mochrie and Stiles have reached new heights. They're simply the best improvisers I have ever seen. With black comic Wayne Brady doing stunning musical improvisations I can't recommend a better way to waste an afternoon...

'Russia held its parliamentary elections last week. The result: it decided to go with a dictatorship' – Jon Stewart, *The Daily Show*.

Sometime in the Noughties a shift occurred in American politics. The majority of Americans stopped watching the major news broadcasting (particularly the rabidly partisan Fox News Channel) and started to watch *The Daily Show*.

Which wouldn't be so surprising if the show was not, in fact, a fake news show shown on the Comedy Channel. But such is the integrity of Jon Stewart, its anchorman and presenter, it's trusted more than the guys supposedly informing America. Go figure.

'A lot of people say that this town is too liberal, out of touch with mainstream America, an atheistic pleasure dome, a modern-day, beachfront Sodom and Gomorrah, a moral black hole where innocence is obliterated in an endless orgy of sexual gratification and greed. I don't really have a joke here. I just thought you should know a lot of people are saying that' – Jon Stewart, hosting the Oscars.

Needless to say, in England Channel 4 snapped into action and showed *The Daily Show* a day after its broadcast in the States. Why lord why?

But thank God they do show it at least. I would challenge anyone to find a funnier satirical show on air, or ever come to think of it.

'London cabbies spend years learning the street layout. In New York, cabbies learn which thermos is for coffee and which is for urine, and which they should drink in front of the passengers' – Jon Stewart.

As Fox News becomes increasingly deranged in its opposition to Obama and his supposed 'socialism', Jon Stewart is often the most effective opposition to Republican (and their deranged, gun-toting Tea Party offspring) scaremongering.

In response to the president of the Catholic League's statement that Hollywood is controlled by secular Jews and 'likes anal sex': **'First, secular Jews don't control Hollywood. Over-representation in Hollywood is not the same as control; if secular Jews controlled it, I'd be on a network and Leno, Letterman, and O'Brien would be on the Animal Planet – you understand what I'm saying? Second, Hollywood doesn't like anal sex. It loves anal sex. I'm telling you, you cannot go to a restaurant there without getting sodomized. And might I add: they know what they're doing' – Jon Stewart,** *The Tonight Show.*

The standard of the writing, considering the show is daily, is astonishing and Stewart has become the conscience of his generation. Lord knows when Bush was in power they needed a conscience. The worry he would lose his bite once Obama was in power has been proved to be unfounded. Though there seems to be times when he's better at defending Obama than his own cabinet. One of the most important and valid comics of our times.

'You know, I hear what you're all saying, but doesn't 'elite' mean good? Is that not something we're looking for in a President anymore? You know what candidates, come with me. I know that elite is a 'bad word' in politics,

and you want to go bowling and 'throw back' a few beers, but the job you're applying for, if you get it and it goes well, THEY MIGHT CARVE YOUR HEAD INTO A MOUNTAIN. If you don't actually think you're better than us, then WHAT THE FUCK ARE YOU DOING?'– Jon Stewart, *The Tonight Show.*

Oh, if you want to squirm check out Stephen Colbert (Stewart's sidekick for many years and now with a Comedy Central show of his own *The Colbert Report*) at the White House Correspondents Dinner where he lays into George W. Bush as Bush watches grim-faced. Colbert does his cod-right-winger persona with devastating accuracy:

> *Of Bush:* 'We're not so different, he and I. We get it.
> We're not brainiacs on the nerd patrol' – Stephen Colbert.

Though I'm still looking on YouTube for the moment when apparently Laura Bush, the president's wife, mouths 'fuck you' at Colbert. It might be one of those urban myths but I choose to believe it...

> 'What's an Amish guy with his hand up a horse's ass? A mechanic'
> – Robin Williams.

Robin Williams was originally from Chicago and raised in a well-off neighbourhood in Detroit. His father was a senior Ford executive who was never home. Robin, enthusiastically ignored by his parents, had the third floor of their mansion to himself. Thus he spent an isolated childhood inventing characters to play with.

> 'Reality is just a crutch for people who can't cope with drugs'
> – Robin Williams.

After attending Julliiard where they asked him to leave after a year as they felt there was nothing they could teach him he hit the comedy clubs like a tornado.

**'Cocaine is God's way of telling you you're earning too much money'
– Robin Williams.**

Getting the lead in the TV show *Mork & Mindy* where he played a motor-mouthed alien who could just about impersonate anything he used the four series to springboard his way to a hugely successful movie career.

**'My God, we've had cloning in the South for years. It's called cousins'
– Robin Williams.**

Lord knows he can be cloying but in *Moscow On The Hudson*, *Good Morning Vietnam* and *Good Will Hunting* he proved he can act as well as he can jest. In his finest movie role he isn't even seen: his vocal genius on *Aladdin* playing the genie is unparalleled, even for Disney.

They just let him go wild on microphone and drew around it. God knows what he was actually like during his cocaine years because clean & sober he's still verbally and mentally flying high.

'Divorce comes from the Latin word divorcerum meaning "to have your genitals torn out through your wallet"' – Robin Williams.

He makes an appearance on the theatre interview show *Inside The Actors Studio* where in the space of around forty minutes he performs at least a hundred and fifty voices. The genius is almost unsettling. Borrowing a scarf from a woman in the audience he improvises eight characters in around forty five seconds. It's well worth hunting down on YouTube. *Live At The Met* is my favourite of his concert movies. You will laugh until strange fluid comes down your nose...

'I was licking jelly off of my boyfriend's penis and all of a sudden I'm thinking: Oh My God, I'm turning into my mother!' – Sarah Silverman.

Last but certainly not least is the hottest comedienne on the planet, Sarah Silverman, a seemingly sweet-natured Jewish-American Princess who says jaw-droppingly outrageous things on taboo subjects such as the Holocaust and race.

'People are always introducing me as "Sarah Silverman, Jewish comedienne." I HATE that! I wish people would see me for who I really am – I'm white!' – Sarah Silverman.

Using an exaggeratedly naive persona she mocks the attitudes behind token liberalism. Coming out with lines such as: 'I don't care if you think I'm racist. I just want you to think I'm thin.' 'Strippers should be role-models for little girls. If only for the fact that they wax their assholes.' 'I was raped by a doctor. Which is, you know, so bittersweet for a Jewish girl.'

**'The best time to have a baby is when you're a black teenager'
– Sarah Silverman.**

Hosting an awards ceremony in front of Paris Hilton, who was about to go to jail for drink-driving, she told the audience that the prison governor was going to paint the bars of Hilton's cell to look like penises 'to make her feel at home.' Her video song shown on the *Jimmy Kimmel Show*, when she was actually *dating* chat-show host Jimmy Kimmel: 'I'm fucking Matt Damon' was a YouTube sensation and won her an Emmy.

'I was curious to see which Courtney Love was going to show up: the smeared-lipstick crazy coke whore or the violent smeared-lipstick crazy coke whore' – Sarah Silverman.

Her show on Comedy Central *The Sarah Silverman Program* is as tough and original as her stand-up movie: *Jesus Is Magic*. Lenny Bruce will be sitting up in his grave applauding.

'You don't call retarded people retards. You call your friend retarded when they're acting retarded'– Steve Carell, *The Office*.

Before I close I wanted to mention Steve Carell and Tina Fey. Well, I just sat through the disappointing movie *Date Night* which was only lifted from its mediocrity by the impro skills of the two stars.

'In a study, scientists report that drinking beer can be good for the liver. I'm sorry, did I say "scientist"? I meant "Irish people"' – Tina Fey.

Tina Fey came through the ranks of Second City impro to become head writer of the notoriously male enclave that is *Saturday Night Live*. Writing the hit movie *Mean Girls*, a brilliant dissection of teenage factions in high school, she was given the green light to write and star in *30 Rock*.

A satire of her days in SNL, casting Alec Baldwin as her egomaniac studio boss, Jack Donaghy.

JACK: I want to thank you. For showing me that I could have a pleasant evening with a woman my age.

LIZ: I'm twelve years younger than you.

JACK: A woman your age then.' – *30 Rock*.

Not since Mary Tyler Moore has there been a character as endearing and funny as Liz Lemon on American TV. In a deliberate strategy the plots are not about men and/or dating but about her struggles to stay sane/normal midst the megalomania and in-fighting of producing a TV comedy show.

LIZ: Why are you wearing a tux?

JACK: It's after six. What am I, a farmer?' – *30 Rock*.

Now starting its fourth series the show is an excellent showcase for Fay's gawky charm. Her chance resemblance to Republican Vice-Presidential candidate Sarah Palin led to her return to *Saturday Night Live* for the election race in 2008; Ms. Palin's Alaskan accent and smiling zealotry was perfectly caught by Ms. Fey's impression.

Steve Carell has been around forever and a day. He was the guy who got picked on by Doctor Evil in *Austin Powers*: 'I'm not dead, I'm just really badly burned, could someone call an ambulance?' and was a regular on *The Daily Show* for five years until he found his natural home in the American version of *The Office:*

'Guess what? I have flaws. What are they? Oh, I dunno. I sing in the shower? Sometimes I spend too much time volunteering. Occasionally I'll hit somebody with my car. So sue me – no, don't sue me. That is opposite the point I'm trying to make' – Steve Carell, *The Office*.

Lord knows the English version of *The Office* was funny but Carell takes the show to new levels by bringing genuine pathos to the role of the office manager. He portrays the role as a total asshole but with a decent human being trying to break out.

'On the streets we didn't have any rules. Maybe one. No kicks to the groin, home for dinner' – Steve Carell, *The Office*.

It's in its fourth series in the States and is consistently awesome. If only his movies (avoid *Get Smart*) were of the same standard. But, at least in *The Office: An American Workplace* he remains a deadpan and subtle joy (surrounded by a brilliant cast I might add).

'Feel what it's like to be in someone else's skin. What does it feel like to be a different race? It feels pretty bad, doesn't it?' – Steve Carell, *The Office*.

I was on a bus in Streatham when I heard a group of black teenage girls speaking in a strange tone. It took me about ten minutes to figure out that they were all speaking in the heightened tone of David Schwimmer from *Friends*: 'HELLO?', 'HAVE WE MET?', 'WE WERE ON A BREAK!', 'ONLY IN PRISON!' That black Londoners would speak like Jewish New Yorkers shows just how great a cultural impact the show had on the UK. It ran for ten seasons from 1994 to 2004, 236 episodes in all, receiving 63 Emmy nominations. It was an instant hit when shown on Channel 4 here in England. The cast, in particular Matthew Perry and Jennifer Aniston, were almost effortlessly brilliant. And the supporting players: Tom Selleck, Giovanni Ribisi, Michael Rapaport, Paul Rudd, Jon Favreau and Hank Azaria to name but a few were amongst the strongest ever featured in a comedy show. Maggie Wheeler's terrific turn as Chandler's occasional girlfriend Janis ('OH MY GOD!') merited a show of her own. I enclose ten of my favourite quotes below. I'd feature a hundred if I had the time. I watched the show avidly the first time round then watched them all again when my son was of an age to understand. I never tired of them. Favourite moment? Jennifer Aniston's drunken 'getting over Ross' scene in the restaurant with the borrowed mobile she tosses into an ice bucket with: 'now THAT's closure!' Beyond perfect comic playing. But to the quotes, enjoy:

> CHANDLER: If I'm gonna be an old, lonely man, I'm gonna need a thing, you know, a hook, like that guy on the subway who eats his own face. So I figure I'll be Crazy Man with a Snake, y'know. Crazy Snake Man. And I'll get more snakes, call them my babies, kids will walk past my place, they will run. "Run away from Crazy Snake Man," they'll shout!".

> CHANDLER: Have you ever wondered if there's a town in Missouri or something named Sample? And then as you're driving to the town there's like, a sign that says, "You're in Sample?"

> MONICA: What's "PLEH?"
> JOEY: That's help spelled backwards so that the helicopters can read it

from the air!

MONICA: Ah...what's doofus spelled backwards?

JOEY: Can I see the comics?

CHANDLER: This is the New York Times.

JOEY: Sorry! *(Politely)* May I have the comics.

RACHEL: Ah that's funny! You're a funny guy, Chandler! And you know what else is really funny?

CHANDLER: *(Hesitantly)* Something else I might have said?

MONICA: You broke a little girl's leg?

ROSS: I know, I feel horrible, okay.

CHANDLER: *(Reading newspaper)* Says here a Muppet got whacked on Sesame Street last night. Where exactly were you around tenish?

MONICA: Joey, they're not real! I start miles beneath the surface of these things, okay? They're fake. See *(Monica squeezes her breast)* Honk honk.

CHANDLER: Wow, it's, it's like porno for clowns.

MONICA: All right people, we're in trouble here. We've only got 12 hours and 36 minutes left. Move, move, move!

CHANDLER: Monica! I feel like you should have German subtitles!

CHANDLER: *(Talking to a lesbian)* Penis, schmenis, we're all people, right? *(The lesbian walks away)*

MONICA: *(Trying to cheer up Joey about getting bad reviews)* Wait, wait, wait, wait, wait one minute. Wait a minute. I believe this will change your mind. *(Reading)* "In a mediocre play, Joseph Tribbiani was able to achieve brilliant new levels of..." continued on page 153... "sucking".

While I'm here could I just mention the 154 episodes of *The Gilmore Girls* I recently sat through in less than a month? I know, I should re-arrange this sentence: 'life...get..a.' But the show, which is repeated on E4, is a fast-paced joy. Lauren Graham and Alexis Bledel play a mother and daughter (Lorelai and Rory Gilmore) from a dysfunctional rich family who live in a small town in Connecticut. The dialogue got so fast they had to add a dozen extra pages to the later scripts or so urban legend tells. The dialogue is the sharpest I've heard in any comedy-drama in my lifetime. Some brief examples:

> **RORY: Do something to make me hate you...**
> **LORELAI: Um, go Hitler?!**

> **LORELAI: I'm mad and needy, and I ended up going out to dinner with my parents, who bickered the whole time about which Beatle is alive and which is dead.**
> **RORY: So where'd they land?**
> **LORELAI: John and Keith are dead. Paul and Bingo are still kicking...**

> **LUKE (Lorelai's on/off boyfriend): Very romantic.**
> **LORELAI: Says the man who yelled 'finally' at the end of *Love Story*.**

> **LORELAI'S INSURANCE BROKER FATHER: Though I tip my hat to the criminal mastermind who actually wrote your insurance policy, you should have come to me first.**
> **LORELAI: I might have guessed the name Shyster McShyster was a clue...**

> **LORELAI: Stop saying mother like that.**
> **RORY: Like what?**
> **LORELAI: Like there should be another word after it...**

> **LORELAI: He's snarky.**
> **SOOKIE (Lorelai's best friend): And sarcastic.**
> **LORELAI: He's snarkastic.**

I will marry Lauren Graham one day. He said unrealistically, forgetting he looks like a morose undertaker who fiddles with his clientele...

But enough about TV and more about:

Funny Movies

I don't think I've ever had a life or, if I have, it's been one spent at the movies watching other people lead more exciting lives. Growing up in Acton we lived five minutes from the Park Royal Odeon and the Ealing Odeon was a ten minute bus ride away. But, of course, it was TV that gave me access to all the old comedy greats.

Before BBC1 became the cookery channel it is today it used to show realms of old movies during the school holidays to keep the school-going masses entertained on the cheap.

Norman Wisdom I could never take to. He made the endearing *Trouble In Store* where he played a cack-handed and accident-prone gimp in an ill-fitting suit who managed to wreck the department store where he worked, whilst singing 'Don't Laugh At Me 'Cause I'm A Fool' in a dubious mid-Atlantic croon. The film was such a big hit he remade it over and over again playing a policeman, milkman, handyman, name it. Normally falling over with his foot in a bucket whilst yelling 'Mr. Grimsdale!' for no apparent reason. Lord knows the films were popular in Albania where, between goat fondling there wasn't a lot to do in the way of entertainment, but not in our house. Though, to be fair, we didn't have a goat either. It was the dreadful schmaltz in his films I found unbearable, even as a child, as Norman saved the orphanage/kid on crutches/girl with one lung. I always found the cloying pathos excruciating. Call me a cynic...

Jerry Lewis gurned for America, seeing Dean Martin go on to be a very fine comedian after he split with Lewis, one wonders why he was with him at all. Though, to be fair, they were supposed to be brilliant live. Seeing Martin look wildly embarrassed as he watched Lewis do his gormless pratfalls makes for gristly viewing.

Eventually Martin tired of Lewis's rampant egomania and delusions of being the Next Chaplin and split for Rat-Packsville. Leaving Lewis to indulge in syrup-dripped pathos which even Norman Wisdom would be ashamed of (see him dressed as a clown picking up the kid in leg-braces whilst sobbing like a banshee – it's beyond grotesque).

Charlie Drake movies...why lord why?

The Three Stooges...why Columbia why?

Carry On movies...kill me now, Sweet Jesus, kill me now and save me having to sit through that crap one more time...

'Shut up, he explained' – Ring Lardner.

I should turn on Danny Kaye like a rabid dog for making so many dull comedies but I'll forgive him anything for *The Court Jester*, his finest hour as a cowardly jester mistaken for a Robin Hoodesque freedom fighter. Do avoid *Hans Christian Andersen* however. Was there ever a more cringing performance of buttock clenching over-earnestness committed to the screen?

Am I the only guy in the world who adores Abbott & Costello? Does this mean I'm a bad person? Critics have long written them off as inferior to Laurel & Hardy at their peak. But who the hell is as good as Laurel & Hardy at their peak? I think Abbott & Costello's 'Who's On First' routine is an absolute classic.

Bud Abbott was the straight man and Lou the hysterical and cowardly fool. Abbott would con or confuse Costello just for the sheer hell of it. They made each other throw up in real life, gambled away fortunes and ended up having their balls merrily squeezed by the IRS in the last years of their lives.

'Who's On First' has Abbott telling Lou that the names of the St. Louis baseball team are all odd: like Who, What and I Don't Know. The mayhem ensues as Costello tries to find out who's on first and second base. I did a pastiche/tribute to the routine in my vaudeville Thirties piece *Backstage*:

FUNNY MOVIES

*The stage of a New York theatre; a married couple: HANNA & HERB
LEIBERMAN, a well-known husband and wife vaudeville act in their
forties, perform in a comedy revue.*

HANNA.   There you are, I been looking all over. Where you been?

HERB.   Saratoga, at the races.

HANNA.   Saratoga?

HERB.   *(Points at paper, laughing)* Boy, they give those horses funny
           names: like Where, When, What –

HANNA.   This is a coincidence: I had a bet on the 2.30 at Saratoga.

HERB.   *(Surprised)* You did?

HANNA.   I can bet on a horse. What am I, a moron?

HERB.   The jury's still out.

HANNA.   So who won the 2.30?

HERB.   *Where.*

HANNA.   At Saratoga.

HERB.   *Where.*

HANNA.   *(Louder)* At Saratoga.

HERB.   *(Louder) Where.*

HANNA.   *(Louder still)* At Saratoga, are you deaf?

HERB.   *Where* won the 2.30 at Saratoga, it's the name of a horse.

HANNA.   *Where* is the name of a horse?

HERB.   Of course.

HANNA.   What came second?

HERB.   *When.*

HANNA.   The 2.30 at Saratoga, what came second?

HERB.   *When.*

HANNA.   *(Louder)* The 2.30 at Saratoga.

HERB.   *When.*

HANNA.   *(Yells)* That's what I'm asking.

125

HERB.	*When* came second, *Where* came first, you'll never guess who came third.
HANNA.	*(Exasperated)* Whatever.
HERB.	How did you know?
HANNA.	Know what?
HERB.	That *Whatever* came third?
HANNA.	*(Yells)* I don't know nothing.
HERB.	You should run for president.
HANNA.	*(To heavens)* Just one punch Lord, that's all I ask.
HERB.	*(Breezy)* I bet on *When*, I won fifty bucks.
HANNA.	Well, that's good.
HERB.	Not so good, I got mugged.
HANNA.	You got mugged?
HERB.	Coming out of Saratoga.
HANNA.	That's bad.
HERB.	Not so bad – the cops caught the mugger.
HANNA.	That's good.
HERB.	Not so good – she's an elderly widow with six kids. Who'll support them while she's in the slammer?
HANNA.	You were mugged by an old woman?
HERB.	She was a very big woman, size of a bull, uglier than Bigfoot.
HANNA.	*(Winces)* That's bad.
HERB.	Not so bad she's got a great personality.
HANNA.	That's good.
HERB.	Not so good, she's got terrible BO.
HANNA.	That's bad.
HERB.	Not so bad, in prison she'll fit right in. But she won't be in there long. She's got a great lawyer.
HANNA.	Well, that's good.

HERB.	Not so good. She's promised to beat the crap out of me soon as she's out of jail.
HANNA.	That's bad.
HERB.	Not so bad, I can afford a doctor, I got money.
HANNA.	You got money, in that suit, who knew?
HERB.	Yeah, I won big at Saratoga.
HANNA.	Ah, *Where*.
HERB.	Saratoga.
HANNA.	No, *Where*.
HERB.	Saratoga.
HANNA.	*Where* won the race.
HERB.	When?
HANNA.	The 2.30.
HERB.	No, you were misinformed, *When* came second in the 2.30.
HANNA.	*(Yells)* Remind me next time we have a conversation: never to have a conversation.
HERB.	What?
HANNA.	Don't tell me: that won the 3.30 at Saratoga.
HERB.	Don't be ridiculous: *What* won the 4.30 at Saratoga.
HANNA.	*(To heavens)* Why Lord, why?
HERB.	Won the Kentucky Derby.
HANNA.	Who did?
HERB.	No, *Why* did. By three clear lengths, it was in all the papers.
HANNA.	*(Exasperated)* Please stop talking.
HERB.	Broke its leg, at Belmont Park, they had to shoot it like a dog.
HANNA.	What broke its leg?
HERB.	No, *Please Stop Talking* broke its leg. *What* won the 4.30 at Saratoga. Didn't I mention it?
HANNA.	*(Tearful)* I want to die.

HERB.   Nah, I don't know a horse with that name. That would be ridiculous.

HANNA grabs him by the lapels of his jacket violently, in exasperation.

HANNA.   *(Yells)* You're giving me a headache.

HERB.   Some nag.

HANNA.   What is?

HERB.   No, *What*'s a great nag, don't get me wrong, but when it comes to horses *You're Giving Me A Headache* is one hell of of a nag, won the 1.30 at Saratoga despite the limp and the hunchbacked jockey.

HANNA.   Better brace yourself.

HERB.   Why?

HANNA.   You're about to get mugged again.

HERB.   By who?

HANNA.   Me.

HERB.   *(Surprised)* Horses mug people?

HANNA.   *(Yells)* There's no horse called 'me'.

HERB.   Hello? *Me* won at Belmont Park in the 3.30, *You* came second, *I* came third.

HANNA.   *(Yells)* I was never in a horse-race.

HERB.   Sure it was, came third.

HANNA.   *(Yells)* I'm going to kill you.

HERB.   For coming in second, are you crazy, it tried its best.

HANNA.   *(Yells)* You're sending me nuts.

HERB.   No, but I might send it some hay.

HANNA.   What's the matter with you?

HERB.   Hello? It's depressed it came second.

HANNA.   Get away from me.

HERB.   I never touched it. My mother always told me: touching horses in certain places is wrong. *(Winks)* You know where.

HANNA.	Where?
HERB.	Won the 2.30 at Saratoga, *When* came second, *Whatever* came third. What are you, deaf?
HANNA.	*(Screams in frustration)* Aaaaaaaaaaaaaaaaaaaaaaaaaaaaah!

HANNA grabs the newspaper from HERB and begins beating him about the head with it, he runs off stage, she following; energetic music plays; a snap blackout.

The problem with Abbott & Costello is they kind of flogged themselves and their own material to death. They made thirty-six films between 1940 and 1956. Including *One Night in the Tropics, Buck Privates, In the Navy, Hold That Ghost, It Ain't Hay* and *Pardon My Sarong*. As well as never being off the radio and having a long-running TV show.

Alright, they were never that choosy about their material but in their best routines: 'Two Tens for a Five', 'Slowly I Turned, Step By Step' and 'Susquehanna Hat Company' as well as the aforementioned 'Who's On First' they created some of the great vaudeville routines of their times.

Ok, like I said, they were no Laurel & Hardy...

OLLIE: Well, here's another fine mess you've gotten me into.'

Watching *Way Out West*, the best of their longer features, as research for this book (it's a tough job but someone has to do it) I was struck by how peculiar it is that Laurel & Hardy ever came together at all. Were there two more different human beings on the planet?

It's not just the sizes: fat guy and thin guy. Listen to their accents. Hardy came from a Southern gentility (his parents ran an upmarket hotel) in Harlem, Georgia and Laurel came from the slums of Ulverston, Lancashire.

They were thrown together by Hal Roach on numerous occasions before Roach and indeed, Stan and Ollie, realised that this was a partnership made in heaven. Laurel had come over with Fred Karno's troupe which included the young Charlie Chaplin. How Laurel must have reacted to Chaplin's astronomical success (at one stage Chaplin could boast he was the most famous man on the planet) is anyone's guess. But Laurel, though a later developer, certainly reached the same comic heights.

OLLIE: Where were you born?

STAN: I don't know.

OLLIE: Fancy not knowing where you were born.

STAN: Well, I was too young to remember.

Most double acts have a stupid guy and a smart guy, not Laurel & Hardy. They were both dumb. They were both likeable characters but capable of extreme violence against themselves and others. Hardy had a dignity and grace of movement which defied his large bulk and, indeed, had a lovely light tenor voice. Laurel had the expressions and movements of a Holy Fool.

STAN: Septober...Octomber...no wonder.

It was normally Laurel's gormless ideas that got them in trouble but Hardy was never far behind when it came to idiocy. His looks to camera of quiet exasperation whenever Laurel got him in trouble one more time were always a joy to behold.

They appeared in many guises: as soldiers, sailors, buskers, foreign legionnaires – but they were always the underdog, taking on the bullies and braggarts; working class/blue collar guys trying to make a buck and normally destroying someone's house or car in pursuit of it...

OLLIE: Well, fan my brow, I'm from the South!

GIRL.: You are?

STAN: Well, shut my mouth, I'm from the South too.

OLLIE: (*Offended*) The South of what, sir?

STAN: The South of London. – Way Out West.

The simple act of delivering a piano was turned into a masterclass of ineptitude and mayhem (*The Music Box*). Laurel always thought they were better in their two-reelers but many of their full-length features: *A Yank at Oxford*, *Way Out West*, *Sons of the Desert* and *Block-Heads*, for example, all stand up extremely well today.

They played England in the Fifties when their film career had dried up and though it wasn't the best of acts the British audiences greeted them with unparalleled affection. They were mobbed wherever they appeared which shows how highly thought of they were in Europe. In real life they were as good and kind men as you would want them to be. Gawd bless 'em.

'Marry me and I'll never look at another horse,'
– Groucho Marx, *A Day At The Races*.

Several years ago I showed *Horse Feathers* to my then twelve-year-old son and he started sneering after about five minutes. 'Who's the old dude doing all those lame puns?' he groaned. I felt like sobbing. He meant Groucho Marx. Groucho had meant so much to me as a kid I always hoped my son would get into him.

My Aunty Jean in Gateshead let us stay up late one holiday to watch *A Night in Casablanca* and though it wasn't the best of their movies (*A Night at the Opera* or *A Day at the Races* take that honour) I was transfixed. The exuberant rudeness of Groucho and the deranged anarchy of Harpo gripped my young imagination.

For the next twenty years or so I was doing Groucho impressions until even I was sick of it. But I did get a play out of it. In this scene from *Schmucks* Lenny Bruce and a young comic Joe Klein meet Groucho Marx in a diner during the New York blackout of 1965:

> *A figure enters the diner, dressed in a yellow rain slicker and hat, dripping with rain. This is GROUCHO MARX, aged seventy-five, slightly stooped but still as sharp as hell in his mind. GROUCHO has seen friends and relatives drop like flies.*

GROUCHO.   Is this a village idiot convention or does everyone look this stupid?

LENNY.   Well, well, well.

GROUCHO.   I know you, you're Bruce.

LENNY.   Call me Lenny.

GROUCHO.   I prefer Bruce. I never use the first name of a man I plan to despise.

GROUCHO strips off the rain slicker and hat. Underneath he wears a dark suit and black tie. He hangs the rain slicker on a peg.

GROUCHO.   I'm soaked through. If it had got any wetter I'd have been mugged by a halibut. *(To JOE)* What are you looking at?

JOE.   You're Groucho Marx.

GROUCHO.   I've heard.

JOE.   I thought you were dead.

GROUCHO.   Not yet.

JOE.   What are you doing in the Village?

GROUCHO.   Slumming, what do you think? It was either this or watch my wife drown in a Martini one more time; are you going to invite me to sit down?

LENNY.   Why the hell not?

GROUCHO sits in the booth, glances around him.

GROUCHO.   Jeez, what a dump.

JOE.   This is incredible: I get to meet Groucho Marx.

GROUCHO.   What's your name, kid?

JOE, thrown by the question and GROUCHO's presence, just stares.

LENNY.   *(Prompting)* Joe.

JOE.   *(Blurts)* Joe Klein?

GROUCHO.   You a comic too?

JOE.   Only – technically.

GROUCHO.   I never heard of you.

JOE.   Me neither.

GROUCHO.   I love humility – in others.

LENNY.   Didn't you used to be in the movies?

GROUCHO.   I was until they started to stink.

LENNY.   Isn't he bitter?

GROUCHO.   You'd better believe it.

> MARY, a waitress, enters, walks over to their booth and places a coffee in front of LENNY.

LENNY.   *(Irish accent)* God bless you, Mary. God bless all the pregnant virgins of the world.

MARY.   Can it. *(To GROUCHO)* You want to order, mister?

GROUCHO.   Black coffee; hold the moo juice.

MARY.   Another big spender, I can't wait for the tip.

GROUCHO.   I never tip.

MARY.   Our cook spits in the coffee of guys who don't tip.

GROUCHO.   Suddenly I tip big.

MARY.   Thought so.

> MARY smiles archly and walks away. GROUCHO stares at her departing frame.

GROUCHO.   If I was forty years younger – I wouldn't touch her with a barge pole.

> GROUCHO takes out a cigar.

LENNY.   Is that an addiction or a prop?

GROUCHO.   Both.

LENNY.   Props are the last refuge of the truly desperate.

GROUCHO.   This from a man who gets his penis out on stage?

LENNY.   We all have our trademarks. You have your cigar: I have my dick.

GROUCHO.   You can take a cigar out in mixed company.

LENNY.   *(Laughs)* Are we going to have fun tonight or what?

GROUCHO.   Why, are you leaving?

Though you have to sit through a lot of lame sub-plot concerning juvenile love affairs or light operatic singers warbling bad songs for no apparent reason the aforementioned *A Night at the Opera* and *A Day at the Races* have held up the best of the Marx Brothers MGM films. Parts of *At the Circus* and *Go West* are great but again you have to sit through a lot of dross to get to the comic gold. I'd gleefully avoid *Love Happy* (which isn't a Marx Brothers movie at all), *Room Service* (which was ineptly adapted from a Broadway play) and *The Big Store*.

Here's a taste of the justifiably famous 'party of the first part' routine:

GROUCHO MARX: Now pay particular attention to this first clause, because it's most important. There's the party of the first part shall be known in this contract as the party of the first part. How do you like that, that's pretty neat eh?

CHICO MARX: No, that's no good.

GROUCHO MARX: What's the matter with it?

CHICO MARX: I don't know, let's hear it again.

GROUCHO MARX: So the party of the first part shall be known in this contract as the party of the first part.

CHICO MARX: Well it sounds a little better this time.

GROUCHO MARX: Well, it grows on you. Would you like to hear it once more?

CHICO MARX: Just the first part.

GROUCHO MARX: What do you mean, the party of the first part?

CHICO MARX: No, the first part of the party, of the first part.

GROUCHO MARX: All right. It says the first part of the party of the first part shall be known in this contract as the first part of the party of the first part, shall be known in this contract – look, why should we quarrel about a thing like this, we'll take it right out, eh?

CHICO MARX: Yes, it's too long anyhow.

(They tear off strips of their contracts.)

CHICO MARX: Now what have we got left?'

GROUCHO MARX: Well I've got about a foot and a half. Now what's the matter?

CHICO MARX: I don't like the second party either.

GROUCHO MARX: Well, you should have come to the first party, we didn't get home till around four in the morning. I was blind for three days.

CHICO MARX: Hey look, why can't the first part of the second party be the second part of the first party, then you'll get something.

GROUCHO MARX: Well look, rather than go through all that again, what do you say?

CHICO MARX: Fine.

(They tear off strips of their contracts.)

GROUCHO MARX: Now I've got something here you're bound to like, you'll be crazy about it.

CHICO MARX: No, I don't like it.

GROUCHO MARX: You don't like what?

CHICO MARX: Whatever it is, I don't like it.

GROUCHO MARX: Well don't let's break up an old friendship over a thing like that. Ready?

(They tear off strips of their contracts.)

CHICO MARX: OK. Now the next part I don't think you're going to like.

GROUCHO MARX: Well your word's good enough for me. Now then, is my word good enough for you?

CHICO MARX: I should say not.

GROUCHO MARX: Well I'll take out two more clauses. Now the party of the eighth part –

CHICO MARX: No, that's no good, no.

GROUCHO MARX: The party of the ninth part –

CHICO MARX: No, that's no good too. Hey, how is it my contract is skinnier than yours?

GROUCHO MARX: Well, I don't know, you must have been out on a tail last night. But anyhow, we're all set now, are we? Now just you put your name right down there, then the deal is legal.

CHICO MARX: I forgot to tell you, I can't write.

GROUCHO MARX: Well that's all right, there's no ink in the pen anyhow.' – A Night At The Opera.

Their earlier Paramount pictures have no plot to speak of but are hugely enjoyable set pieces and Woody Allen swears that *Duck Soup*, their 1934 satire on politics and war, is a masterpiece so who am I to argue?

'Military intelligence is a contradiction in terms' – Groucho Marx.

I'm still puzzled why Chico Marx, a Jewish-German from New York, felt compelled to speak in a cod-Italian accent and why Harpo chose to not speak at all but, hey, why fight success?

'I never drink water, fish fuck in it' – W.C. Fields.

I find W.C. Fields movies pretty unwatchable frankly but the alcoholic misanthrope attitude of the man slays me. His 'anyone who hates dogs and children can't be all bad' persona was a glorious throwback to a Dickensian age. In fact, he played Mr. Micawber in the Thirties MGM movie of *David Copperfield* remarkably well.

In the Thirties on radio he had a famous running 'feud' with Charlie McCarthy the ventriloquist dummy worked by Edgar Bergen where they gleefully hurled insults at one another:

> **W.C. FIELDS: Well, Charlie McCarthy, the woodpecker's pinup boy!**
>
> **CHARLIE: Well, if it isn't W.C. Fields, the man who keeps Seagram's in business!**
>
> **W.C. FIELDS: I love children. I can remember when, with my own little unsteady legs, I toddled from room to room.**
>
> **CHARLIE: When was that? Last night?'**
>
> **W.C. FIELDS: Quiet, Wormwood, or I'll whittle you into a venetian blind.**
>
> **CHARLIE: Is that your nose or are you eating a tomato?**

W.C. FIELDS: Tell me, Charles, is it true that your father was a gate-leg table?

CHARLIE: If it is, your father was under it.

W.C. FIELDS: Why, you stunted spruce, I'll throw a Japanese beetle on you.

CHARLIE: Why, you bar-fly you, I'll stick a wick in your mouth, and use you for an alcohol lamp! Pink elephants take aspirin to get rid of W. C. Fields.

W.C. FIELDS: Step out of the sun Charles. You may come unglued.

CHARLIE: Mind if I stand in the shade of your nose?

It was a shame Rod Steiger, a man with no noticeable sense of humour (if he had one he hid it well) played Fields in the Seventies movie *W.C. Fields and Me*. Because he was totally unfunny: if only a comic had played the role (same with Dustin Hoffman as Lenny Bruce of course).

Fields was the same person off stage and on. He took an unfeasible pride in his lawn outside his mansion but unfortunately he lived next door to Nelson Eddy, the light operatic singer, who had a large and unruly collection of exotic birds. Nelson Eddy came out of his house one morning to find Fields enthusiastically shooting flamingos from the sky with a pellet gun. 'What the hell are you doing?' yelled Eddy. 'I'm going to keep shooting the bastards until they shit green,' replied Fields.

This is the guy who first coined the phrases: 'I drink therefore I am', 'I am free of all prejudices: I hate everyone equally', 'if you first don't succeed, try, try again then quit; no point being a dang fool about it'; the man who wanted his epitaph to be: (he was born in Philadelphia but loathed it) 'Here lies W.C. Fields. I would rather be living in Philadelphia.' It would have been fantastic to see his act; which began life as a juggling turn but the sardonic asides took over; one of the greats.

'Drown in a cold vat of whisky? Death, where is thy sting?' – W.C. Fields.

I never took to Bob Hope as a comic. He was more a joke machine. Hope was the smug voice of the establishment and, in the case of the Vietnam War, the voice of the military. He'd lost touch with his audience by the late Sixties and was booed at the Oscars for anti-hippy/draft dodger remarks.

'Give me a lemonade.' (*The whole rough gold-prospector bar goes quiet; he snarls:*) 'In a dirty glass!' – Bob Hope, *Road To Utopia*.

BUT check out his films from the Forties and his work with Bing Crosby in the *Road To...* movies where he perfected the cowardly braggart routine to a fine art. In many ways it's a shame he was the other guy because before his films became lazy and unpleasant in the Fifties and Sixties (watching a sixty-year-old fat guy chase nubile girls in bikinis is a tad revolting, ask Benny Hill) he made some brilliant comedies.

INDIAN GUIDE: Aren't you scared of big, empty houses?

HOPE: Not me, I've played Vaudeville.

Check out *Road to Utopia* and *Road to Morocco* that he made with Crosby, the two Western parodies *The Paleface* and *Son Of Paleface* he made with Jane Russell, the haunted house pictures *The Cat and the Canary* and *The Ghost Breakers* and the thriller spoof *My Favorite Brunette*.

Being chased by a ghost in a suit of armour, glances at camera: 'Anyone got a tin opener?' – Bob Hope, *The Ghost Breakers*.

Woody Allen was hugely influenced by Hope in his early movies. He reworked the cowardly womaniser shtick for Seventies audiences. Of course, I'm one of the people Woody despises, in that I prefer his early funnier films: *Take the Money and Run*, *Bananas*, *Love and Death*, *Sleeper*, *Every Thing You Always Wanted To Know About Sex*, *Annie Hall* and *Manhattan* are as good movies as any comic ever made...

'I object your honor! This trial is a travesty. It's a travesty of a mockery of a sham of a mockery of a travesty of two mockeries of a sham'
– Woody Allen, *Bananas.*

The Fool trying to open the Queen's chastity belt:
'With most grievous dispatch I shall open the latch to get at her snatch'
– Woody Allen, *Every Thing You Always Wanted To Know About Sex.*

'I'll get broads up here like you wouldn't believe: swingers, freaks, nymphomaniacs, dental hygienists...' – Wood Allen, *Play It Again Sam.*

'My Grammy never gave gifts. She was too busy getting raped by Cossacks' – Woody Allen, *Annie Hall.*

When I was living in Newcastle I went to see on two Saturdays running: *Young Frankenstein* and *Monty Python and the Holy Grail.* I think I reached a level of comic Nirvana that week that I never reached again. I was fifteen years old. It was all downhill from there.

Why Mel Brooks didn't keep writing with Gene Wilder is a mystery because *Young Frankenstein* is his subtlest and most complete film.

FRANKENSTEIN (Gene Wilder): Grab the bags.

IGOR (Marty Feldman): Ok, you take the blonde, I'll take the brunette.

The Producers is a gleeful slice of bad taste. I prefer the original to the musical but each to their own taste and it was a funny evening at the theatre *if* you forgot about the original movie.

'Actors are not animals! They're human beings!'
'They are? Have you ever eaten with one?' – *The Producers.*

National Lampoon's Animal House introduced us in Europe to the wild and demented comic talent that was John Belushi. I saw the movie in a cinema on a Sunday night in Devizes, Wiltshire, the night when they showed 'uncommercial movies' and the audience went nuts for Belushi. Not having got *Saturday Night Live* in the UK he was an unknown quantity. I always prefer his performance in *Animal House* and find *The Blues Brothers* overrated.

Incidentally, watching *National Lampoon's Animal House* again I was blown away by Tim Matheson's performance as the womanising Otter. He should have done more comedy (though he was great in Mel Brooks' remake of *To Be Or Not To Be* as Anne Bancroft's lover).

Such was the brilliance of the film I expected much more of *National Lampoon* but all they gave us after that was lame vacation movies with the dead-eyed Chevy 'I'm Only Here For The Pay Cheque' Chase. Belushi succumbed to his heroin addiction and something was lost.

TED STRIKER: My orders came through. My squadron ships out tomorrow. We're bombing the storage depots at Daiquiri at 1800 hours. We're coming in from the north, below their radar.

ELAINE DICKENSON: When will you be back?

TED STRIKER: I can't tell you that. It's classified. – *Airplane.*

Airplane was a revelation when it came out in the Eighties. 'Don't call me Shirley,' entered the playground lexicon. The joy of the *Airport* spoof was getting straight actors like Robert Stack, Lloyd Bridges and Leslie Neilsen (*Forbidden Planet, Earthquake*) to send themselves up in deadpan style. Neilsen in particular found an entire new career with *The Naked Gun* spoofs.

'Looks like I picked the wrong week to quit sniffing glue'
– Lloyd Bridges, *Airplane.*

I am normally the first one to run out of the cinema screaming if I'm forced to watch a rom-com but the funniest rom-com ever made might just be *When*

Harry Met Sally, which incidentally brought Harry Connick Junior's music to world attention; Billy Crystal, a fine comic, found an ideal vehicle for his talents (something he has seldom done since) and Meg Ryan was ditzy charm itself. The woman who quips 'I'll have what she's having' after the fake orgasm scene was Rob Reiner's mother by the way; and there was great support from Carrie Fisher and Bruno Kirby as the sidekicks.

> **'You know, I have a theory that hieroglyphics are just**
> **an ancient comic strip about a character called Sphinxy'**
> **– Billy Crystal, *When Harry Met Sally*.**

Bill Murray first came to prominence in *Caddyshack* playing a stoner golf course groundsman trying to get rid of a gopher. Not one of the subtlest movies in the world but he was very good and hit the big time with *Ghost Busters*. The latter movie hasn't aged well but his perfect performance comes in *Groundhog Day*. I saw it on its release in 1992 and didn't really register just how good the film was. It's one of those movies that reputation grows with the passing of years.

It's a simple premise, an obnoxious news reporter is sent to cover groundhog day in a small New England town and starts to live the same day over and over again. Why this should be is never explained but once you accept the premise the film becomes funnier and funnier. Particularly with Murray's constant attempts at suicide, when he knows no matter what he does he will wake up in the same crummy rooming house listening to the same inane banter of local DJs. He's finally saved by his love for Andie McDowell. Murray's deadpan desperation is actually highly touching and, save in *Rushmore* and *Lost In Translation*, he was never as good again. Kill to see *Rushmore*, by the by, Murray competes with a nerdy schoolkid for the love of a schoolteacher and is a bilious delight.

> **Speaking to a rich kids school assembly: 'You guys have it real easy. I**
> **never had it like this where I grew up. But I send my kids here because the**

fact is you go to one of the best schools in the country: Rushmore. Now, for some of you it doesn't matter. You were born rich and you're going to stay rich. But here's my advice to the rest of you: Take dead aim on the rich boys. Get them in the crosshairs and take them down. Just remember, they can buy anything but they can't buy backbone. Don't let them forget it. Thank you.' – Bill Murray, *Rushmore*.

I subscribe to the general belief that *Life of Brian* is the funniest movie ever made, which brings me back to the Pythons of course. I didn't think *Monty Python and the Holy Grail* could be topped but they did it.

> **JONES: *(With a sweep of his hand towards the window)* One day, lad, all this will be yours...**
> **PALIN: What, the curtains?' – *Monty Python and the Holy Grail*.**

The soundtrack of *Life of Brian* is almost as funny as the movie itself. Their comedy albums (largely masterminded by the ever industrious Eric Idle) were hugely influential on me and my brother as kids. In a skit deleted from my play *Pythonesque* I have Cleese enter a record shop in search of the Python cannon:

CLEESE.	Excuse me is this the shop where one might purchase CDs of a comedic bent?
PALIN.	*(Shifty shopkeeper)* Sometimes.
CLEESE.	What is it other times?
PALIN.	A front for a brothel; you're not a copper's nark, are you?
CLEESE.	Not in the least.
PALIN.	I was gored by a nark once; those antlers are vicious.
CLEESE.	That's of no consequence now. I've been imprisoned in a Vietnamese prisoner-of-war camp since 1975 and being recently released, the bamboo pole still firmly inserted up my anus, thought I might revisit the Monty Python albums I used

	to find so very, very amusing in my youth. Do you happen to stock the Monty Python cannon?
PALIN.	Absolutely, there's a huge call for them. They never go out of fashion do they, they're so very, very witty. Yes, surrealism never dates.
CLEESE.	Goodo. Do you happen then to possess a copy of their self-titled debut?
PALIN.	Not at the moment, sir.
CLEESE.	Ah, well, would you have the classic *Another Monty Python Record*?
PALIN.	Very funny that one, laugh a minute, sobbed with laughter listening to that one I did.
CLEESE.	Yes, but do you have it?
PALIN.	Not in stock at present, sir.
CLEESE.	Very well, how about *Matching Tie and Handkerchief*?
PALIN.	Ah, lovely album; got the cheese shop sketch on it, and Oscar Wilde. 'One of Shaw's, sir.' A classic of its kind.
CLEESE.	I'd rather hear it myself than listen to you paraphrase it thank you.
PALIN.	Sold the last one this morning, sorry sir.
CLEESE.	*Monty Python's Previous Record*?
PALIN.	Had one.
CLEESE.	But?
PALIN.	It got stolen, by a Liverpudlian.
CLEESE.	*Live at Drury Lane*?
PALIN.	Oh yes, got that one, absolutely.
CLEESE.	Let's have it then.
PALIN.	*(Ducks under counter then returns)* Sorry, sir, the mice ate it.
CLEESE.	How could mice eat a CD?
PALIN.	They're very big mice, sir; actually they're iguana.

CLEESE.	*The Album of the Soundtrack of the Trailer of the Film of Monty Python and the Holy Grail*?
PALIN.	Not much call for that one, sir.
CLEESE.	Not much call? It's one of the great comedy albums of our times.
PALIN.	Not in these parts, sir.
CLEESE.	*Monty Python Live at City Center*?
PALIN.	The one where they sing *Sit on my face and tell me that you love me*?
CLEESE.	That's the one.
PALIN.	Sold the last copy to the leader of the Conservative Party; this very morn.
CLEESE.	You're sure you actually stock Monty Python CD's?
PALIN.	Absolutely.
CLEESE.	*Monty Python's Contractual Obligation Album*?
PALIN.	No.
CLEESE.	*The Monty Python Instant Record Collection*?
PALIN.	Yes or, then again, no.
CLEESE.	*Monty Python Sings*?
PALIN.	Not anymore they don't.
CLEESE.	You don't have any CD's of Monty Python at all do you?
PALIN.	You haven't asked about the soundtrack to the *Meaning of Life* yet.
CLEESE.	Is there any point?
PALIN.	Who dares wins, sir.
CLEESE.	Do you have it?
PALIN.	Not in the least.
CLEESE.	You've wasted my time entirely.
PALIN.	That'd be the point, sir.
CLEESE.	I see.

PALIN.	How about a bunk up with a Chinese bint for only thirty-seven guineas instead?
CLEESE.	Oh, alright then.

Why there was a huge religious objection to *Life Of Brian* is beyond me. If they had treated Jesus with anything else but respect and love the zealots crusading against the film might have a point. But the film was an attack on religious intolerance and sectarianism. Though parts of *The Meaning of Life* are glorious (the exploding fat bastard, the 'Every Sperm Is Sacred' musical sequence, the organ donations against your will skit), *Life Of Brian* is the Python's crowning glory. My particular favourite character being Mike Palin's apologetic centurion sending people off to die: 'Crucifixion? Oh good...' Terry Gilliam designed the movie, by the by, and it outshines any Biblical movie you can think of for authenticity. Also perhaps because it is set in Biblical times it's a movie that's never dated.

> **BRIAN: Excuse me, are you the Judean People's Front?**

> **REG: Fuck off! We're the People's Front of Judea! – *The Life Of Brian*.**

Well, that's me lot. There's a hundred comedy movies I should have mentioned that I've adored over the years, but to quote twenty five:

> *Dr. Strangelove:* 'Gentlemen, you can't fight in here! This is the War Room!

> *Ten Things I Really Hate About You:* 'The shit hath hitith the fan... ith!'.

> *Juno:* 'Doctors are sadists who like to play God and watch lesser people scream.'

> *The Fortune Cookie:* 'Why don't you kids go play on the freeway?'

> *The Odd Couple:* 'I can't take it anymore, Felix, I'm cracking up. Everything you do irritates me. And when you're not here, the

things I know you're gonna do when you come in irritate me. You leave me little notes on my pillow. Told you 158 times I can't stand little notes on my pillow. "We're all out of cornflakes. F.U." Took me three hours to figure out F.U. was Felix Ungar!'

Bringing Up Baby: 'Now it isn't that I don't like you, Susan, because, after all, in moments of quiet, I'm strangely drawn toward you, but well, there haven't been any quiet moments.'

The Jerk: 'Good Lord – I've heard about this – cat juggling! Stop! Stop! Stop it! Stop it! Stop it! Good. Father, could there be a God that would let this happen?'

My Favourite Year: 'Catherine, Jews know two things: suffering, and where to find great Chinese food.'

Being There: 'It's for sure a white man's world in America. Look here: I raised that boy since he was the size of a piss-ant. And I'll say right now, he never learned to read and write. No, sir. Had no brains at all.
Was stuffed with rice pudding between the ears, short-changed by the Lord, and dumb as a jackass. Look at him now! Yes, sir, all you've gotta be is white in America.'

Midnight Run: 'I just got two words to say to you: shut the fuck up.'

Diner: 'You know what word I'm not comfortable with? Nuance. It's not a real word. Like gesture. Gesture's a real word. With gesture you know where you stand. But nuance? I don't know. Maybe I'm wrong.'

Its A Mad Mad Mad Mad World: 'As far as I can see, American men have been totally emasculated – they're like slaves! They die like flies from coronary thrombosis while their women sit under hairdryers eating chocolates and arranging for every second Tuesday to be some sort of Mother's Day! And this positively infantile preoccupation with bosoms. In all my time in this wretched Godforsaken country, the one thing that has appalled me most of all: this preposterous preoccupation with bosoms. Don't you realize they have become the dominant theme in American culture: in literature, advertising and all fields of entertainment and everything. I'll wager you anything you like that if American women stopped wearing brassieres, your whole national economy would collapse overnight.'

Tin Men: 'You found God in the smörgåsbord?'

His Girl Friday: 'Now, get this, you double-crossing chimpanzee: there ain't going to be any interview and there ain't going to be any story. And that certified check of yours is leaving with me in twenty minutes. I wouldn't cover the burning of Rome for you if they were just lighting it up. If I ever lay my two eyes on you again, I'm gonna walk right up to you and hammer on that monkeyed skull of yours 'til it rings like a Chinese gong!'

This Is Spinal Tap: 'We're very lucky in the band in that we have two visionaries, David and Nigel, they're like poets, like Shelley and Byron. They're two distinct types of visionaries, it's like fire and ice, basically. I feel my role in the band is to be somewhere in the middle of that, kind of like lukewarm water.'

Catch 22: 'Ok, let me see if I've got this straight. In order to be grounded, I've got to be crazy. And I must be crazy to keep flying. But if I ask to be grounded, that means I'm not crazy anymore, and I have to keep flying.'

South Park – Uncut: 'And now back to Wild Animal World. Here in the more arid regions of Africa, the Gold Coast lions are in the throes of mating season. The male lion positions himself behind the female and prepares to insert his lionhood. Notice, his large swollen balls; the female lion relaxes her body and says "hello" to Mr. Winky. The male lion is enticed by the female's supple breasts and firm backside. Quickly and suddenly the male is finished. So, he kindly asks the female to leave. He promises he'll call her tomorrow. But the female doesn't leave. Nope, she's moving right in. Looks like the male lion... is screwed.'

The Philadelphia Story: 'I thought all writers drank to excess and beat their wives. You know one time I secretly wanted to be a writer.'

Arthur: 'I race cars, play tennis, and fondle women – but I have weekends off and I am my own boss.'

The Princess Bride: 'The King's stinking son fired me, and thank you so much for bringing up such a painful subject. While you're at it, why don't you give me a nice paper cut and pour lemon juice on it? We're closed.'

Withnail & I: 'I don't advise a haircut, man. All hairdressers are in the employment of the government. Hairs are your aerials. They pick up signals from the cosmos, and transmit them directly into the brain. This is the reason bald-headed men are uptight.'

What's New Pussycat: 'We played strip chess. She had me down to my shorts and I fainted from tension.'

Little Miss Sunshine: 'You know what? Fuck beauty contests. Life is one fucking beauty contest after another. You know, school, then college, then work, fuck that. And fuck the air force academy. If I wanna fly, I'll find a way to fly. You do what you love, and fuck the rest.'

Trains, Planes & Automobiles: 'You know everything is not an anecdote. You have to discriminate. You choose things that are funny or mildly amusing or interesting. You're a miracle! Your stories have NONE of that. They're not even amusing ACCIDENTALLY! "Honey, I'd like you to meet Del Griffith, he's got some amusing anecdotes for you. Oh and here's a gun so you can blow your brains out. You'll thank me for it." I could tolerate any insurance seminar. For days I could sit there and listen to them go on and on with a big smile on my face. They'd say, "How can you stand it?" I'd say, "'Cause I've been with Del Griffith. I can take ANYTHING.'"

Some Like It Hot: 'Nobody's perfect!'

But time waits for no man and I've run out of time so let us journey forth, with a heavy heart and possibly comedic indigestion, to the epilogue:

What Has Comedy Ever Done For Us?

(In the style of Les Dawson please):

In 1812 during the epic, snow-chaffed retreat from Moscow the crestfallen and embittered Napoleon Bonaparte, fleeing from the Cossack hordes who were harrying and cutting down the stragglers of his once proud Imperial army, halted his half a million men in the mud and sleet and stared forlornly down at the scorched earth of Mother Russia. Not one man moved as the snow fell and the frostbite bit into the bare arms and legs of that ragged, wretched and defeated host.

Finally General Nay, Bonaparte's finest commander and hero of Austerlitz, edged his horse forward towards his Emperor and in polite tones asked if anything was wrong. 'Nobody move,' Napoleon said. 'I think I've lost a contact lens.' Which has nothing to do with me leaving the stage but it just goes to show how your mind wonders when you're trying to get off with a laugh.

When I think of my life comedy runs through it. Through all the ups and downs comedy and comedians has been there for me. Keeping me sane in a savage world. Making failure and disappointment somehow, against all the odds, bearable. That's what comedy does for us. That's what it will always do. So let's hear it for all the comedy monkey boys and girls who've kept misery and despair away from my door: shine on Stan Laurel and Oliver Hardy... shine on Abbott & Costello & 'Who's on First'...shine on Groucho, Chico and Harpo & 'the party of the first part'...shine on Eric Morecambe and Ernie Wise, who always brought me sunshine...shine on Norman Stanley Fletcher, Rigsby, Reginald Perrin, the Likely Lads... shine on Judd Hirsch, Danny De Vito, Andy Kaufman... shine on The Banana Splits, Pinky & The Brain, Atom Ant...

shine on Bugs and Daffy and Foghorn, Tweety Pie and Sylvester... shine on the Ant Hill Mob, Dastardly and Muttley, Professor Pat Pending...shine on Basil Brush, Lamb Chop, ALF... shine on the Lad Himself, Dave Allen, the Goodies, Monty Python's Flying Circus... shine on Captain Mannering, Sergeant Wilson, Private Pike...shine on Frank Spencer...shine on Ralph Malph and the Fonz... shine on F-Troop... shine on Top Cat and Ernie Bilko and Scooby Doo... Fred & Barnie, Wilma, Betty and Bam-Bam... shine on Steve Martin and Steven Wright and Robin Williams... shine on Chris Rock and Bill Cosby and Billy Crystal... shine on Les Dawson... shine on Spike Milligan and the glorious, god-like Goons... shine on Jasper Carrott and Billy Connolly... shine on Chic Murray and Stanley Baxter... shine on Kenneth Williams and Sidney James and Hattie Jacques... shine on Eric Sykes and Tommy Cooper and Dick Emery... shine on Rowan & Martin, Rhoda Morgenstern, Carol Burnett... shine on Victoria Wood, Julie Walters, Joyce Grenfell, the Liver Birds... shine on Bill Bailey, Lee Mack, Linda Smith... shine on Bob Newhart, shine on Woody Allen and shine on Richard Pryor, Lenny Bruce and Bill Hicks, who walk with the comedy angels... shine on, shine on, shine on... now and forever. For without laughter what are we but walking ghouls?

'Say goodnight Dick.'
'Goodnight Dick!' – Rowan & Martin.

The End

PS Five favourite jokes that didn't make it:

'What do you get when you cross a homosexual with a Jew?
(Sings) A Broadway show!'

'What do you get when you cross George Formby with Eddie Murphy?
(Formby voice) "Turned out nice again, motherfucker!"'

'How many psychiatrists does it take to change a light-bulb? Only one but the light-bulb has to want to change.'

'A bear and a rabbit are having a shit in the woods. The rabbit says: 'How do you wipe your arse without toilet paper?' The bear says: 'I always do this' picks up the rabbit and wipes his arse with it...'

'Buddy Holly's not really dead he's on another plane.'